The Christi Money

LEGACY PRESS®
www.LegacyPressKids.com

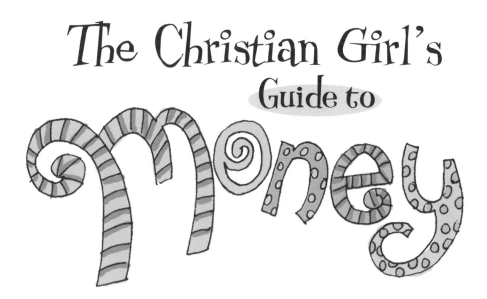

The Christian Girl's Guide to Money

Rebecca Park Totilo

To my daughter and best friend, Rachel, to whom I owe a debt of gratitude for helping me research and test lots of moneymaking ideas, as well as contributing to this book by adding today's Christian girl special touch. You're the greatest!

To my husband, Mark, and the boys: Dylan, Dallas and Judah. Thanks for giving Mama the space, time and break from the kitchen!

And very special thanks to Joe and Wilma Jo Arrington for allowing me to retreat to their quiet hideaway in the mountains of North Carolina, where I finished this project. As fellow writers, you know how much that meant!

THE CHRISTIAN GIRL'S GUIDE TO MONEY

©2012 by Rebecca Park Totilo, fourth printing
ISBN 10: 1-58411-067-8
ISBN 13: 978-1-58411-067-5
Legacy reorder# LP48215
JUVENILE NONFICTION / Religion / Christianity / Christian Life

Legacy Press
P.O. Box 261129
San Diego, CA 92196
www.LegacyPressKids.com

MIX
Paper from
responsible sources
FSC® C048831

Cover Illustrator: Anita DuFalla
Interior Illustrator: Aline Heiser

Scriptures are from the *Holy Bible: New International Version* (North American Edition), ©1973, 1978, 1984 by the International Bible Society. Used by permission of Zondervan Bible Publishers.

Printed in the United States of America

TABLE OF CONTENTS

Dear Christian Girl 9

Chapter 1: Money, Money, Money, Money, Money! 11
   Quick Quiz! Where Is Your Heart? 13
   Hey, Big Spender 15
   Miss Pursestrings...16
   The Greed Weed...17
   I'm Puzzled! Richly Blessed.............................18
   Don't Worry, Be Happy! 19
   Bee-Attitudes of Good Stewardship 19
   Make It! Washington Quarter Necklace 22
   I'm Puzzled! Called By Any Other Name 23
   Takin' Care of Business: Poor Rich!.................24

Chapter 2: Money Management 101 27
   Let Me Introduce You 28
   Miss Pursestrings...31
   Make It! The One Dollar Ring 33
   Pledge, Then Plan 34
   Money Counts Up 36
   Build Your Budget 38
   I'm Puzzled! Face Up to It 39
   The Envelope, Please 40
   Takin' Care of Business: The Three Daughters 41

Chapter 3: Be a Savings Sleuth! 45
   Dialing for Dollars 47
   Net Savings...48
   Miss Pursestrings...49

Water Works 50

Feed Your Wallet 51

The Heat Is On 52

Don't Let the Electric Slide 53

Takin' Care of Business: Honesty Still Pays 54

Chapter 4: Give It Away 57

Offer It Up..59

For Richer or for Poorer 60

Make Me an Offering..60

Miss Pursestrings 61

When to Give 62

Quick Quiz! Why Do You Give? 63

I'm Puzzled! Do U Luv Money? 65

Giving Project 65

Donations 66

Takin' Care of Business: A Love Offering..................66

Chapter 5: A Penny Saved 69

Go for the Goal 70

Miss Pursestrings..71

Make It! Miss Piggy Bank 72

You Can Account on These 75

Dealing with Cards 77

Money Adds Up 78

Bartering..80

Quick Quiz! Sav-o-meter...80

Takin' Care of Business: The Generous Woman............82

Chapter 6: Spend Some! 85

Needs Vs. Wants..86

Miss Pursestrings..87

Good Buying...89

I'm Puzzled! Mug Shots 91

Smart Shopper 92

Quick Quiz! Deep Sea Spending 93

The Price Is Right 96

Avoid Spending Pitfalls...97

Make It! Snap Dragonfly Money Clips 98

Battling Bad Spending Habits 99

Takin' Care of Business: The Big Spender 100

Chapter 7: Work It, Girlfriend! 103

Show Me the Money!..105

Quick Quiz! The Sky Is the Limit 105

Make a Schedule 109

Miss Pursestrings...110

A Nice Price 111

Which One Are You? 113

Help Wanted: Partnering With a Friend 114

Takin' Care of Business: Purple Thread 114

Chapter 8: Open for Business!..117

The Name Game 118

Location, Location, Location 119

A Good Start...119

Make the Right Call...120

Let Your Fingers Do the Walking....................................121

Get the Word Out..122

Miss Pursestrings...123

Tools of the Trade 124

Do's and Don'ts for Successful Business Owners.............126

Dress for Success 127

Sales 101 127

I'm Puzzled! Work It Out 128

Takin' Care of Business: Something Borrowed 128

Chapter 9: Fun Ways to Earn Cash 131

Extra Stuff 186

DeAR CHRISTIAN GIRL,

It's a funny thing, me writing a book about money. Me, the big spender! The more I can buy with what little I have, the better. You can find me digging in a bin of clearance items! Don't get me wrong, though. I don't love money – just using it.

When I was about your age, my thoughts were preoccupied with where or when I could get more money – so I could spend it. One day my mom said, "If you want something, you are going to have to work for it." So I found myself trying all sorts of moneymaking schemes and businesses in hopes of striking it rich!

I dreamed of someday becoming a millionaire. When I told my mom that, she crinkled a smile and said, "Yeah, right." I guess she knew that someone who enjoyed spending and giving away money as much as I did would easily go through a million bucks! She knew I'd never hold onto it long enough to count it.

So how does someone like me reach her goal if she never saves a dime?

Maybe you're like me. You know, one of those people who walks around with only a few pennies in her pocket or purse. I guess you could say the five-second rule applies here (you know the one: if you drop a piece of candy on the ground, it is still good for five seconds). Of course, in this case, given five seconds, people like me will spend all of our money. Money seems to burn a hole in our pockets.

Not that this is always bad. If I saw someone on the street corner who needed money, I would give it to him or her. Who can pass up the opportunity to do something for God's kingdom? People who like to spend usually make great bargain-hunters, too, and can sniff out a sale a mile away. You know the type: catch all the off-season sales, then save our purchases for later. Folks like me view money as a vehicle to get what we want, not an end in itself.

Maybe you are just the opposite. You have saved every penny you ever received as a birthday gift or earned mowing lawns. I have a lot of respect for people who are disciplined in their spending and stash away money in their piggy banks. Some people, though, don't want to spend any of their money. They are called "misers" and are considered tight-fisted because they struggle with giving. The money channel gets stopped up with them. I have to admit, there have been times when I have needed to get the plunger and do some "Drano™ work" on my giving to get the blessings flowing, too.

Neither of these cases is really wrong, except when taken to the extreme! God wants us to be all of these: thrifty shoppers, hard workers, great savers and generous givers for His kingdom. This book will help you discover more about how to be balanced in all of these things; plus, how to be a good steward over the money He provides for you. And, in practicing these principles, it is my prayer that you will realize your childhood dreams, as I have mine.

Join me on this journey, as we discover together all the ways to make money, save money, invest money and spend money!

YOUR FAITHFUL STEWARD,
Rebecca Park Totilo

10

CHAPTER ONE

MONEY, MONEY, MONEY, MONEY. MONEY!

Everyone needs it, everybody wants it and everyone enjoys having lots of it! But green backs (another way to say "money") are really just fancy paper with green ink. So what's the big attraction? Why is money such a big deal for most people?

You might think that money will give you more control over your life. But, in fact, just the opposite is true. Often, people with a lot of money are the least happy and least successful people around. Why? Because they think their moolah (yet another way to say "money"!) makes them safe from bad things so they no longer need to stay close to God. And they are plagued with worry over the possibility of losing their precious money. The money they thought would bring them peace of mind ends up burdening them with sleepless nights! There are many stories of big jackpot winners who end up as homeless people because they gave money the wrong place in their lives.

By the way, being rich is more than just having stacks of cash to count. God gives you other blessings, too, such as talents and time, that He wants you to use wisely. So even if you never have a lot of money, you're not off the hook with God. He's looking for you to use whatever you have to do His will.

So how do you pull this off? How can you be the master of money in your life? Here are three ways:

☀ LISTEN TO GOD ☀

Pray and ask Him to open your eyes so you know the right and wrong ways to handle the blessings He gives you.

12

❄ READ THE BIBLE ❄

God's Word speaks very plainly (and loudly!) about money. In fact, the Bible has more than 2,000 verses related to money!

❄ FOLLOW THE TIPS IN THIS BOOK ❄

The more you learn about money, the better you will be at handling it.

GOD WANTS YOU TO RULE MONEY, NOT SERVE IT.

By being in charge of the financial circumstances in your life, you will be free to make the right choices and solve your money problems with God's help.

WHERE IS YOUR HEART? ❄

Circle **T** if the statement describes you or something you have done, or **F** if it does not.

T OR F **1.** You keep every dime you can get your hands on. No one knows your stash is buried under your mattress.

T OR F **2.** Your closet is overflowing with every toy and gift you have ever received. You even have a stuffed animal your brother won for you at the county fair when you were three. Your mother is begging you to get rid of some things!

T OR F **3.** Before the holidays, your youth group is filling up shoe boxes with toys, books and pencils for a poor child in another country. You put some stuff in yours, but you keep the really cool fuzzy pencil for yourself.

T OR F **4.** When your favorite group comes out with a new CD, you dash off to the music store to buy it.

T OR F **5.** All of the popular girls at school shop at expensive stores, so to keep up with them you spend every penny you have to get an outfit like theirs.

T OR F **6.** Church friends encourage you to volunteer at the thrift store, but you'd rather get a real job that pays big money.

T OR F **7.** Your brother wants to go hang out with friends, but he has to mow the lawn. You offer to do it, but only if he pays you $20.

T OR F **8.** You leave your wallet at home on purpose because the church is taking up a special offering for missionaries in China. You know if you bring it, you'll feel guilty and give in just in time for the passed plate.

T OR F **9.** When your class has a food drive, you dig out of the back pantry a can of spinach you hate and won't miss.

T OR F **10.** You buy lots of stuff at yard sales even though you don't need it. Everything is so cheap!

COUNT THE ANSWERS YOU MARKED "FALSE", THEN TURN THE PAGE!

7 or More F's: Your heart is looking good! There are only a few weak areas you need to work on. Keep on exercising those giving muscles and take a dose of God's Word once a day.

4 to 6 F's: Your pulse is a bit weak, and your heart is beating a little below average. You may need more loving oxygen in your blood. Drink one glass of God's presence along with two prayer pills before bedtime.

3 or fewer F's: Uh-oh! It looks like your arteries are clogged with the love of money. Go directly to the Master Surgeon. Ask Him to perform surgery on your heart and help you to be more generous.

❋ HEY, BIG SPENDER ❋

Even though kids your age usually don't have regular jobs and incomes, they are viewed as a huge sales market! You and your friends are part of an age group that spends $150 billion each year and influences another $150 billion of your parents' spending. You offer your say on everything from fashion and entertainment to big-ticket items like cell phones and cars. But you're also careful with your money: three out of four kids your age say they shop at retailers known to have low prices, and 73 percent say they look for sales.

So where are kids your age getting their money? In national surveys, almost half (48 percent) of those asked said they get an allowance from their parents, while almost as many (43 percent) reported that they are paid for jobs they do for non-family members (such as babysitting, pet sitting or yard work). And one in three teens (35 percent) said they have a regular job. Wow! The average preteen girl spends $50 a week, about $24 of which is her own money. The most popular item to buy is clothing. Does that really surprise you?

Dear Miss Pursestrings,

A girl who sits next to me in school is always asking me for money. She says she forgot it or lost it. And I can never say no! Yesterday, I saw her eating pizza and fries at lunch, while I ate a PB&J sandwich from home. I worked so hard to earn this money by grooming my neighbors' pets – she's making me really mad! And to top it all off, she never pays me back. What should I do?

Sincerely,
Lo Ner

Dear Lo,

I understand why you wouldn't want to loan any more money to her – she's forgetting that a loan is not a gift! Have courage to stand up to her and say no the next time she tries to borrow from you. Say something like this: "I can't loan you

any more money because you haven't paid me back." If you notice her asking other classmates for money, tell your teacher. Someone needs to stop this girl before she bankrupts your whole class!

Miss Pursestrings

Dear Miss Pursestrings,

My parents say playing the lottery is a waste of money. I think it would be great to win a zillion dollars. What's so bad about playing a little game with the chance to win money?

Sincerely,
Ima Winner

Dear Ima,

Your parents are right. Proverbs 13:11 says, "Dishonest money dwindles away, but he who gathers money little by little makes it grow." When you work hard to earn money, you can make it grow by investing, saving or spending it on things you need. The lottery attracts people with the false hope that they will become rich instantly, without working for it. But many people who win the lottery actually end up broke after just a few years because they don't know how to manage their money. God wants you to work hard and manage your money wisely.

Miss Pursestrings

☀ THE GREED WEED ☀

The Bible says that the love of money is the root, or beginning, of all evil (1 Timothy 6:10). When you love money (or your possessions) more than God, those things become your "god"…and that's when the greed weed starts to grow. As you think more about money and less about God, the greed weed starts to choke your relationship with God. These uncontrolled cravings for saving, earning and spending money actually leave you a spiritual pauper! Some people even break God's laws just to make more money.

In Luke 12:15, Jesus said, "A man's life does not consist in the abundance of his possessions." He wasn't saying that having money and possessions is a bad thing. It's when you allow money to distract you from God and His Word that the trouble starts. That's why Jesus asked His followers, "What good will it be for a man if he gains the whole world, yet forfeits his soul?" (Matthew 16:26).

As a believer in God, you don't want to let greed grow in your heart and choke out your love for Him and His Word. It's up to you to  choose where you are going to put your attention: God or money. Matthew 6:24 says, "No one can serve two masters. Either he will hate the one and love the other, or he will be devoted to the one and despise the other. You cannot serve both God and money." You can't be devoted to both! Money promises things it can't deliver. Stick with the one who will "never leave you or forsake you" (Deuteronomy 31:6). Put your money on God!

I'm Puzzled! RICHLY BLESSED

Find out about someone who was rewarded for obeying God. Use the words below to fill in the blanks in the Scripture.

gold	livestock	everything	Egypt
Lot	wife	wealthy	Abram	silver

So _____ went up from _____ to the Negev, with

his _____ and _____ he had, and _____ went

with him. Abram had become very _____ in _____

and in _____ and _____. (Genesis 13:1-2)

☀ DON'T WORRY, BE HAPPY! ☀

Our Heavenly Father promises to take care of our daily needs with food, clothing and shelter. You don't have to worry about your need for more. Luke 12:22-23 says, "Therefore I tell you, do not worry about your life, what you will eat; or about your body, what you will wear. Life is more than food, and the body more than clothes." Jesus said not to set your heart on those things, because God already knows that you need them. Instead, you are to follow Him, and you will receive everything you need – and maybe some things you just plain want, too!

Good Cents Scripture

And my God will meet all your needs according to his glorious riches in Christ Jesus.

~ Philippians 4:19

☀ BEE-ATTITUDES OF GOOD STEWARDSHIP ☀

Being a good steward means being a faithful manager over what God has given you. You can "bee" a success by putting the following principles to work for you – the Bible says so! Buzz by these tips to find out more about good stewardship.

Bee aware that God owns everything.

The earth is the Lord's, and everything in it, the world, and all who live in it.

PSALM 24:1

Bee a good manager and take care of all He has placed you over.

Whoever can be trusted with very little can also be trusted with much, and whoever is dishonest with very little will also be dishonest with much. So if you have not been trustworthy in handling worldly wealth, who will trust you with true riches? And if you have not been trustworthy with someone else's property, who will give you property of your own?

LUKE 16:10-12

Bee a giver. God loves when you give generously.

Honor the Lord with your wealth, with the firstfruits of all your crops; then your barns will be filled to overflowing.

PROVERBS 3:9-10

Bee content with your circumstances – no matter how rich or how poor.

For I have learned to be content whatever the circumstances. I know what it is to be in need, and I know what it is to have plenty. I have learned the secret of being content in any and every situation, whether well fed or hungry, whether living in plenty or in want. I can do everything through him who gives me strength.

PHILIPPIANS 4:11-13

Bee a help to those with needs.

If anyone does not provide for his relatives,

and especially for his immediate family, he has denied the faith and is worse than an unbeliever.

1 TIMOTHY 5:8

Bee free by staying debt-free.

The rich rule over the poor, and the borrower is servant to the lender.

PROVERBS 22:7

Bee prepared for emergencies.

In the house of the wise are stores of choice food and oil, but a foolish man devours all he has.

PROVERBS 21:20

Bee in prayer about your finances, in times of plenty and times of want.

Our Father in heaven, hallowed be your name, your kingdom come, your will be done on earth as it is in heaven. Give us today our daily bread. Forgive us our debts, as we also have forgiven our debtors.

MATTHEW 6:9-12

Bee responsible by doing things God's way and following His plan.

But seek first his kingdom and his righteousness, and all these things will be given to you as well.

MATTHEW 6:33

 **Make It!** # WASHINGTON QUARTER NECKLACE

Wear this pendant to celebrate President's Day, July 4th, Memorial Day, Veteran's Day or any time you're feeling patriotic!

What You Need

star patterns on page 186

shiny quarter

red, white and blue construction paper

glue

2–3 feet yarn (red, white or blue)

scissors

hole punch

What to Do

 1. Using the star patterns, cut out three stars (one red, one blue, one white).

 2. Glue the medium-sized star onto the biggest star, then glue the smallest star on the medium star. You should see a color border around each star.

3. Glue a quarter face-up in the middle of the smallest star.

4. Punch a hole near the top of the biggest star. Thread the yarn through, forming a necklace, and tie.

CALLED BY ANY OTHER NAME

What is your favorite way to say "money"? Circle the words below that have been used to describe money.

Oscar	Script	Simoleon
Mazuma	Plaster	Scratch
Bacon	Dough	Lucre
Legal Tender	Bills	C-note
Bread	Ace	Bones
Bean	Boffo	Case Note
Coconut	Fish	Frog Skin
Lizard	Peso	Rock
Yellow Back	Bullet	Skins
Casholah	Payola	Green Backs
Big Bucks	Smackers	Cold Hard Cash
Clams	Moolah	Iron Man
Plug	Sinker	Wagon Wheel
Sour Dough	Rhino	Spondulicks

Answer: All of the above, with the exception of "Sour Dough," which is a slang term for counterfeit money.

TAKIN' CARE OF BUSINESS
Poor Rich!
(Based on Matthew 19:16-22)

There once was this absolutely gorgeous guy named Rich. Oh, and did I mention he was popular AND wealthy? Anyway, he had everything a guy could want: plasma TV, video game system, state-of-the-art computer – you name it, he had it. All the girls at school had a crush on him. He was one lucky guy.

Then one day, Rich ran into Jesus coming down the road. He was glad to see Jesus because he had a question for Him.

"I want to live forever," Rich said. "I wouldn't want this world to have to go on without me."

Jesus rolled His eyes. He knows a fake when He sees one. (Just ask Judas!)

Rich was impatient. "So where can I get a good deal on eternal life?" he persisted. "I've heard it's really expensive, but that's no problem. I'm loaded."

"Why are you asking Me about buying eternal life?" Jesus asked patiently. "God doesn't take cash, or even credit cards. If you want eternal life, you need to obey His commandments."

"What commandments?"

"You know, the Ten Commandments," Jesus said. "And you must love your neighbor."

"I've done all that," Rich answered. "I've been a good kid all my life. What else?"

"OK, show Me that you mean what you say," Jesus said. "Sell all your stuff and give the money to charity. Then come and follow Me."

"Aw, man," Rich said as he shook his head with disappointment. "I love my stuff. I don't want to sell it." And he went home, miserable.

To Think About!

Has God ever required you to give up something?

Prayer

Dear God, sometimes I think that in order to serve You, I have to give up everything and live as a very poor person. I admit it, I don't want to be poor. I want to be rich! I know from reading the Bible that if I obey You, You will bless me with riches beyond just money or things. Please help me to know that money is not the best thing: You are. I love You more than money. Amen.

Green Back FACT

Have you every left a dollar in your pants pocket, then thrown your pants into the washer? The dollar comes out all nice and clean! Did you wonder why paper money doesn't disintegrate like a movie ticket might? It's because, unlike normal paper, such as notebook paper or newspaper, money is made from rags. This is also known as "rag paper" or "fine linen writing paper." Rag fibers bond together much better than fibers in regular paper. So, just like fabric, money is unaffected by water.

$ CHAPTER TWO $

MONEY MANAGEMENT 101

You may have heard that budgets are like diets – they don't work! But that's simply not true. A budget isn't like one of those one-week diets where you suffer through cabbage soup to lose a few pounds, then return to ice cream later. Instead, a budget sets you on a course for life. This cool tool will help you track your spending and allow you to set goals for your money. A budget will actually encourage you to make changes in the way you live so you can have the money you want when you need it.

At first, a budget might feel like Delilah's Super Cuts to your Samson-ite wallet, sapping all of your spending strength. But if you hang in there, you will see your saving muscles grow, empowering you with financial freedom. In no time, you will be watching those pennies pile up!

☀LET ME INTRODUCE YOU☀

If you want money to be your friend and not your enemy, you need to get to know it first. Have you ever looked at a paper bill and wondered what all of that stuff means? Well, step right up and let me introduce you. You might be surprised at all of the Christian symbolism in our friendly dollar bill!

Nifty Thrifty Tip

Save money on movie rentals by checking them out at your local library. It's free!

The first dollar bills with their current design were printed in 1957. They are made from a blend of cotton and linen (but they don't need ironing!). Look for the tiny red and blue threads woven into them.

The letter in the left center circle stands for the location of the Federal Reserve Bank that issued the bill. There are 12:

A Boston	G Chicago
B New York	H St. Louis
C Philadelphia	I Minneapolis
D Cleveland	J Kansas City
E Richmond	K Dallas
F Atlanta	L San Francisco

Whoever is the treasurer of the United States at the time the bill is printed gets to have his or her signature on every bill.

Every bill has a different serial number, such as this one.

This is the year that the bill was designed.

This is the U.S. Treasury Seal. The scale on top stands for a balanced budget. The carpenter's square, which is in the middle, is used for an even cut. It stands for fairness. At the bottom is the key to the U.S. Treasury.

The two circles together make up the Great Seal of the United States.

The words "Annuit Coeptis" are Latin for "He [God] has favored our undertakings." "Novus Ordo Seclorum" is also Latin and means "A new order for the ages" – a reminder of America's recent separation from Britain. The pyramid stands for strength, and the eye above it represents God watching over us. The reason the eye piece was kept separate from the pyramid was to show that with God's help, all can be achieved. At the base of the pyramid are the Roman numerals MDCCLXXVI, which means 1776, the year the Declaration of Independence was signed.

The eagle is the symbol of the United States. It represents strength. The banner in the eagle's beak says "E Pluribus Unum," which is Latin for "out of many, one." The 13 stars and stripes on its shield represent the first 13 states, or colonies. The eagle holds an olive branch and arrows in its claws to show that Americans want peace, but we're ready to fight. It faces its left talon to show that the U.S. favors peace over war.

The number 13 shows up over and over again on the dollar bill:

❋ **13 STARS** above the eagle

❋ **13 STEPS** on the pyramid

❋ **13 LETTERS** in "Annuit Coeptis"

❋ **13 LETTERS** in "E Pluribus Unum"

❋ **13 BARS** on the shield

❋ **13 LEAVES** on the olive branch

❋ **13 FRUITS** on the front

❋ **13 ARROWS** in the eagle's right claw

Dear Miss Pursestrings,

While I was in line at a store last night, a blind lady in front of me made a purchase using cash. She knew exactly what to give the cashier. I was amazed that no one had to help her. How was she able to tell the difference between $5, $10 and $20 bills?

Sincerely,
Countess Cash

Dear Countess,

I'll bet if you closed your eyes you'd be able to distinguish between coins, because they are different sizes. Quarters and dimes have ridges around them, while pennies and nickels are smooth. Paper money is a little different. Some blind people keep their money in different pockets for different bills. One common way to tell paper money apart is to fold the bills in different ways. A $10 bill could be folded longways, while a $5 bill might be folded in half twice the short way. Did you happen to hear the lady ask the cashier what change she was handing back to her? Sometimes, when they get money back, they ask which bill is which and then fold it. Try it at home sometime.

Miss Pursestrings

Dear Miss Pursestrings,

Why do people sometimes give the cashier more money than they should when they are buying something? Yesterday, the man in front of me gave the clerk a $5 bill plus three pennies, but the total was only $4.98! I know I'm no math genius, but I don't get it.

Sincerely,
Penny Pinch

Dear Penny,

That's a great question! Sometimes, people like to get rid of the extra change in their pockets – especially pennies, which can really weigh them down. In this case, the man gave the clerk $5.03 so he could get a nickel back in change ($5.03 - 4.98 = .05). That way he only had to carry one coin – a nickel – instead of two pennies. Cashiers don't mind making change because the cash registers do the math and tell them how much to give back, and they can always use the pennies to make change for their other customers.

Miss Pursestrings

Make It!

THE ONE DOLLAR RING

Impress your friends by wearing this on your finger!

What You Need

1 clean, crisp $1 bill

What to Do

1. Fold down the white border frame (the entire length along the top and bottom only) of the bill toward the face on the front of the dollar.

2. Now, neatly fold the bill in half twice (lengthwise). You should be able to see the "1" on each side.

3. Choose one end, and fold the white border back. Now, fold this same side, with the "1" back toward the other side, so that it is framed evenly in a square. This end will be called the "top" and the other end will be called the "bottom."

4. Holding onto the top folded end, rub the dollar over a table's edge to make your bill form a circular shape.

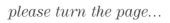

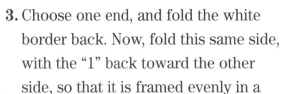

please turn the page...

5. With the top folded "1" facing up, make a 90 degree bend in the dollar around the first letter in the word "one." Where you make this bend will determine the size of your ring - so you may need to adjust it a bit by wrapping it around your finger to find the best fit. (Note: the farther out from the bent down end, the larger the ring.)

6. Fold the bottom half down over the 90 degree corner, forming an upside down "L" shape.

7. Now, curve the top end with the "1" back around to position on top of the 90 degree corner just made.

8. Open the top of the framed "1" and wrap the bottom around the body of the ring until all of the excess length is used, then fold the top back down and tuck under the white frame border to hold it in place.

9. Once you have mastered this, trying using 5s, 10s, or even $20 bills!

☀PLEDGE, THEN PLAN☀

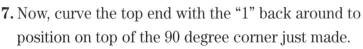

Before you set up a budget, it is important that you commit to staying within the limits you set for yourself. In other words: no cheating! It's easy to buy something on impulse – like those cute little hair clips you saw last week while waiting in line at the drugstore – and then justify it later. But impulse buys are budget busters, so for heaven's sake (and I do mean that!), avoid them!

How can you protect yourself against impulse buying? First, remember that feelings follow actions. Your heart will follow and do what is right once you put your mind to it. It will take strong determination, but you can do it! Second, do the obvious: leave your

Nifty Thrifty Tip

Dying to try that new lip gloss color? Ask for a free sample at a department store cosmetic counter.

money at home! Sure, you'll want to have what you need for what you're doing, but don't carry extra money with you. If you see something you really want, you always can come back and buy it

later. But chances are, by the time you get home, you'll decide you really didn't want that purple pen or dangly earrings or neon nail polish so bad after all.

This "wants" and "needs" thing can be tricky, by the way. One of the great things about growing up is getting to make some of your own decisions – but that also means taking on responsibility. Every time you spend money, you will have to weigh one item against another. Ask yourself: Is this something I really need? Can I live without this for now? If I buy this, what am I not going to be able to buy later?

It sometimes can be hard to answer these questions when you're standing near the checkout counter at your favorite department store, with your emotions racing. So stop, take a deep breath and think about it. If you are still unsure, ask God to help you. And even if you do make your purchase and regret it later, you can always buckle down and start budgeting again. After all, no one is perfect – except Jesus!

Good Cents Scripture

The Lord will guide you always.

~ Isaiah 58:11

☀MONEY COUNTS UP☀

Here are the top 10 ways to live on a budget.

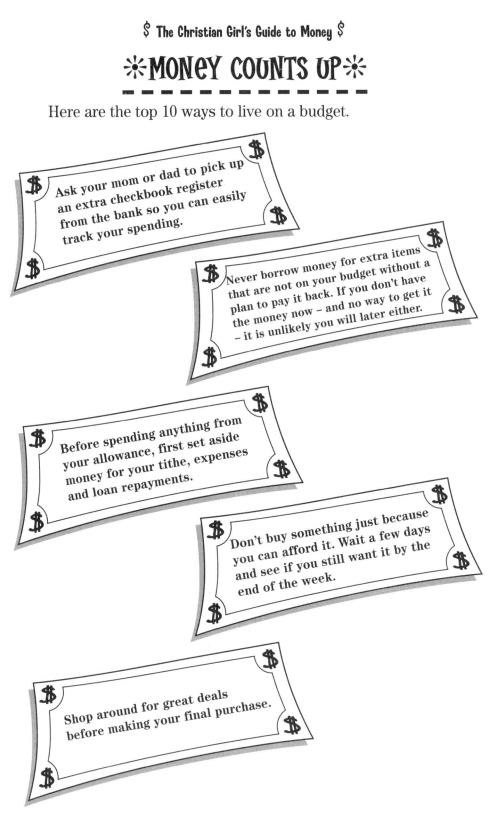

Ask your mom or dad to pick up an extra checkbook register from the bank so you can easily track your spending.

Never borrow money for extra items that are not on your budget without a plan to pay it back. If you don't have the money now – and no way to get it – it is unlikely you will later either.

Before spending anything from your allowance, first set aside money for your tithe, expenses and loan repayments.

Don't buy something just because you can afford it. Wait a few days and see if you still want it by the end of the week.

Shop around for great deals before making your final purchase.

Use coupons to save on purchases. Some stores even double your coupons, which is twice as nice!

Try trading for what you want instead of spending money. Ask your neighbor if you can babysit her kids in exchange for some piano lessons.

Set up a weekly amount for spending on small items such as candy, soda and other snacks.

When an expense is due, pay it right away. You might be tempted to spend the money on something else, but it is more important to get your obligations out of the way first.

Open a savings account at your local bank. Most banks have special accounts for kids that don't charge fees.

❋BUILD YOUR BUDGET❋

Each month, use the My Monthly Budget form on page 187 to track the money you earn (income) and the money you spend (expenses). Start by filling in each type of income you receive. Total these up and this will be your total monthly income.

Now, to figure out how much to set aside for expenses, start by writing in your tithe first. Your tithe should be 10 percent of your total income (divide your income by 10 and tithe 1 part of that – 10 percent of $10 is $1). Next, pay yourself by putting 10 percent into savings. Finally, fill in the rest for lessons, school supplies, loans, dues or other expenses you have. Try to be realistic when figuring how much to set aside for each section.

Figure out what to put in the "What's Leftover" section by subtracting your expenses from your income. This remaining money is your "surplus." What will you do with it? That's up to you. There are some ideas listed there for you, but use the blank lines to fill in your own special goals.

Using this form will help you see how much money you have, where it is going and the best way to reach your goals. But don't be afraid to ask mom or dad for help when you're working out your budget. They probably have lots of experience with stretching their income to fit all of their – and your – expenses.

Green Back FACT

In the U.S., there are three towns named "Greenback," three that are "Dollar," four that are "Buck" and three that are "Bucks." The people in those towns are really in the money!

Good Cents Scripture

Do not let this Book of the Law depart from your mouth; meditate on it day and night, so that you may be careful to do everything written in it. Then you will be prosperous and successful.

~ Joshua 1:8

I'm Puzzled! FACE UP TO IT

How well do you know your coins? Take a look at each pair and circle the coin that has the president facing the correct way. The answer is at the bottom of the page.

Answer: The penny faces right. The nickel, dime, quarter and half-dollar face left.

❋The ENVeLOPe, PLeASe❋

Besides developing a monthly budget, you will want to keep track of your daily earnings and expenses. Sound complicated? Nah! All you need are some plain envelopes and a pen – and you're ready to go!

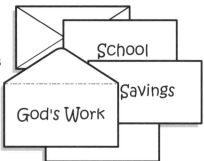

Get an envelope for each of your budget categories and write that budget item on the outside. For example, you might have envelopes for God's Work (tithes and offerings), Expenses (business supplies), Things for Me (personal fun money), School/Classes (dues, fees), Savings, Major Purchases and Other (for Christmas gifts, birthday gifts, etc.). Find a box or drawer to store your envelopes so you have easy access to them.

Now, let's suppose you had a hot dog stand and you sold six hot dogs at $2 a piece. After taking out the cost of your supplies (hot dogs, buns, signs), you walk away with $12 dollars. What do you do with your $12 profit? Pull out your envelopes. First, put $1.20 (10 percent) in your "God's Work" envelope to cover your tithe. Next, put another 10 percent ($1.20) in your Savings envelope. Do the same for the Things for Me envelope. That leaves $8.40. Divide this money according to what you have budgeted for other expenses, and put it in the envelopes you have for those items.

This is where that responsibility thing comes in. If you just started your budget and you know you that have club dues coming up soon, you will want to make sure you have enough in your School/Classes envelope to cover that expense. You may even need to pad it a bit by adding a few extra dollars from this week's earnings. Otherwise, you will have to borrow from another envelope to pay for it, which is not a good habit to get into. But be sure to make a note on the outside of an envelope if you ever do need to borrow from it. The next time you get paid, you will have to pay back that envelope.

Nifty Thrifty Tip

Want to actually see your money grow? Instead of using envelopes, use jars. Place them on your dresser or desk. When you bring home your money, put it in your jars according to your budget.

The hardest part of budgeting and using the envelope system is getting started. But once you do, it gets easier as you go. Give it a few months and you'll see that these envelopes are not so hard to lick after all!

TAKIN' CARE OF BUSINESS
The Three Daughters
(Based on Matthew 25:14-30)

Mrs. Boots had an apple orchard. She also had three daughters to help her tend the orchard.

On Tuesday mornings, Mrs. Boots would take a crate of apples into town to Apple Treats, their small fruit stand by the road. She gave each of her daughters a job to do while she was gone. Margie, her oldest daughter, had 10 rows of apple trees to tend. Her middle daughter, Jo Anna, had four rows of apple trees to tend. And Susan, her youngest, had two rows of apple trees to tend.

"While I'm gone," said Mrs. Boots, "I want you to pick the ripe apples off each of your trees."

"Yes, ma'am," they said.

After Mrs. Boots had driven down the gravel road, Margie quickly gathered all her ripe apples in baskets and took them into the house. She washed them and made apple juice to sell at Apple Treats. Jo Anna gathered all her ripe apples and took them into the house to make apple pies for selling at the stand. Susan watched her older sisters doing all this extra work. But instead she went out to her rows and picked the ripe apples and ate them, throwing the cores away one by one.

When Mrs. Boots returned, she went to see what each daughter had done. Margie showed her a refrigerator full of fresh apple juice.

"You did a good job!" she congratulated. "I will give you more responsibilities."

Jo Anna opened the pantry to show her apple pies sprinkled with cinnamon.

"Those look great!" Mrs. Boots said as she patted her on the back. "I will give you more responsibilities."

Susan said, "I picked all the ripe apples, just like you told us. I ate the apples and threw away the cores."

"But Susan," Mrs. Boots said, "you could have taken the seeds out of the cores and used them to grow more trees. You have not been faithful over these few things. I can't give you more responsibilities."

This story is based on Jesus' parable of the talents. It shows that as God's servants, we should be faithful to His blessings. We shouldn't take for granted that He doesn't care what we do with our time, energy and possessions. He does! In fact, Jesus said if we are faithful over the little things, we will be faithful over big things, too.

God wants us to use all of our talents. Is there anything at which you're really good? Maybe you're a good artist, or a soccer player, or maybe you're good at math. God gave each of us gifts and talents, and He wants us to use them.

To Think About!

How have you been a good steward over the things God has given you?

Prayer

Thank You, God, for all the gifts and talents You have given me. Show me how to use them wisely and be a good manager over my property. In Jesus' name, amen.

Green Back FACT

Think you can print your own money? Think again! Many have tried, but the US Bureau of Engraving and Printing has found ways to combat counterfeiting. For example, the $20 bill has several safeguards. One is the "20" in the lower right corner that is written in color-change ink. There is also a security strip embedded in the paper to the left of Andrew Jackson's portrait, which is only visible when you hold the bill up to the light. Another feature includes micro-writing, a watermark made of closely-spaced lines behind Jackson's face, making it impossible to reproduce – it can only be seen under a microscope!

$ CHAPTER THREE $

BE A SAVINGS SLEUTH!

This book has a lot of tips for helping you become a better money manager. But did you know you can help your whole family save money? By making a few simple changes, your family could save a few dollars a month or more! And who knows? Maybe some of that savings might trickle down to you in the form of extra allowance!

To find out where your family can save, you will need to take on an investigation. So, put on a long, dark coat and grab a magnifying glass and…oh, wait, wrong book! Nah, all you need to do is find some paper and a pen and follow these steps:

❋ LOOK AROUND THE HOUSE AND FIND WASTE ❋

❋ FIGURE OUT HOW TO FIX THE PROBLEMS YOU FIND ❋

❋ MAKE A LIST OF SUGGESTIONS ❋

❋ CALL A FAMILY MEETING AND SHARE YOUR FINDINGS ❋

❋ CHECK AGAIN IN A MONTH TO SEE HOW ❋
THE CHANGES LOWERED THE BILLS

Have you looked around your house and you can't find any ways to save money? Here are some ideas to help you hunt down waste.

☀DIALING FOR DOLLARS☀

That phone hanging on the wall may seem like a piece of furniture, but your family is paying for its service. Depending on the company your parents chose, your family may be paying a monthly charge plus fees for long distance, voice mail, caller ID and other features. Because there are so many companies that offer phone service, there is heavy competition. And when there is competition, you have a chance to save money!

Be a Phone Sleuth!

Ask mom or dad to teach you how to read the phone bill. Explain that you will investigate ideas for changes and give them to your parents, but that you will not make the changes yourself.

Check with your phone service provider to see if you have the cheapest plan available for the types of services you need.

Look for special phone service deals on TV or in the newspaper. Check them against your current plan to see which is the better offer.

Does your family pay for services, such as caller ID, that no one is really using? Suggest that you drop any that are not useful.

Ask if you can look over the bill every month and check it for possible mistakes, such as calls your family didn't make, extended call times or phone numbers your family doesn't recognize.

See if there are any calls that could have been avoided by using email, faxes, or snail mail.

Buy a family address/phone book to put beside the telephone. Fill it in with the names and phones numbers of each family member's favorite call list (relatives, neighbors, favorite pizza take-out, etc.), to avoid using the costly 411 information service.

Does anyone in your family have a cell phone? If so, follow these same steps for cell phone service.

☀NET SAVINGS☀

Over a third of Americans have a computer with Internet service in their homes. Your family may be included in this statistic! If so, you will want to investigate if your family has the best service for your needs.

Be an Internet Sleuth!

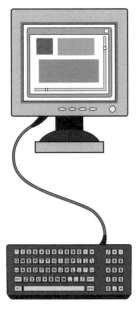

Figure out how much your family uses the Internet. Some services charge by the hour and others charge a flat fee for unlimited usage, so you need to figure out what makes sense for your family.

Find Internet providers who try to "hook" you by offering free service for 45 days, hoping you will stay with them. Try these different services for free for a while to save a little dough.

Even better: use the Internet at your local library. It's free!

Dear Miss Pursestrings,

My family never has any extra money to do anything! I don't even get an allowance. My friends always have plenty of money to do things. How can I get some money?

Sincerely,
Mo Money

Dear Mo,

Why not suggest to your friends that when you hang out together you do things that don't cost money? You also may want to ask them if they would like to help you start a consignment shop, selling all the toys and clothes you can't use anymore. You can earn extra money and have fun at the same time!

Miss Pursestrings

Dear Miss Pursestrings,

Last night, my mom and dad announced at dinner that everyone would be getting only one or two nice gifts instead of the typical eight or nine things at Christmas. They said we needed to cut back on our spending so they could use the leftover money to invest in a college plan for me. But already? I'm not even in high school yet!

Sincerely,
Holly Blue

Dear Holly,

I know you are probably disappointed that you had to shorten your Christmas wish list, but receiving a few nice things is actually better than a lot of cheaper items that might not last through the year. Your parents are smart to invest in your future. It takes years to plan and save enough for college, so now is a good time to start! Your parents will probably put the money they don't spend on gifts into an account for it to grow and earn interest (more money!). Eventually, as your parents add to it each year, your college fund will grow. By the time you are ready for college, the fund will be large enough to help you pay tuition. Now that's a special gift!

Miss Pursestrings

☀ WATER WORKS ☀

Have you seen the "Water Works" space on the Monopoly™ board game? Every time you land on it, you have to pay its owner. That's pretty much how it is in the real world, too – water isn't free. The more you use, the more you pay! Even if you are lucky enough to have a spring-fed well, you still need to conserve water and help save the environment by not watching water go down the drain.

Be a Water Sleuth!

Ask your family to help by making sure they completely turn off the faucet each time they use it.

Check for leaks inside the house and outside at water hose spouts. Tell your parents what you find. Don't forget to check under cabinets to see if pipes are wet or dripping.

If you have lawn sprinklers, ask if they can be adjusted so they don't spray as often or as long.

Take showers instead of baths – a shower uses less water (if you don't hog it for an hour!).

Make sure the dishwasher is full before running it. Not only will you use it less often that way, it works better when it's full.

Try to use the dishwasher instead of hand-washing the dishes. Most dishwashers are designed to use limited water.

☀Feed Your Wallet☀

With all of your family's busy activities – church, school, work, clubs, teams – you might eat at restaurants more than at home. But eating out also eats up your family's money! The good news is this is an area where your family can save a fortune by making some changes in how you eat away from home.

Be a Restaurant Sleuth!

Try using a notebook to keep track of your family's restaurant visits over the next month. Every time you eat out, write down where you eat and how much you spend. At the end of the month, show your parents the results. They might be surprised – and you might find yourself bellying up to the dining room table a little more often!

Watch for restaurant coupons and ask if you can keep them in the car for handy savings.

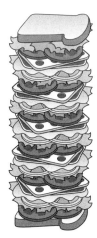

Take advantage of specials at your favorite places, such as 2-for-1 sandwiches.

Order from the kids' menu if you still fit the age group. You might feel older inside, but just think of the money you're saving on the outside!

Pass on that pricey soda and ask for a free cup of water instead.

Good Cents Scripture

But remember the Lord your God, for it is he who gives you the ability to produce wealth.

~ Deuteronomy 8:18

☀ THE HEAT IS ON ☀

Staying warm in the winter can be very costly. Heating bills are one of the biggest "budget gobblers" around! You can help keep your family from burning too much cash on heat.

Be a Winter Weather Sleuth!

On a cold day, check around the windows and doors in your house to see if you can feel air coming in. If you do, tell your parents about the leak – filling it will keep in your heat.

Make sure all doors and windows are closed completely to keep in the heat. A door left open for just a few minutes can let in enough cold air that your furnace has to do double duty.

Most furnaces have filters. Furnaces with clean filters require less energy. Make up a chart so your parents can keep track of when the filters need to be changed.

Ask if you can turn down the heat at night. After all, you will be in a warm, cozy bed. Let the furnace have a little extra rest, too!

☀DON'T LET THE ELECTRIC SLIDE☀

Every light, TV, stereo, DVD player, microwave, computer and clock in your house is burning up green backs. How many times has one of your parents said, "Don't leave that light on!"? Your parents do that because they see the electric bill every month and they know it costs your family money if you waste electricity.

Be a Power Sleuth!

Start turning off lights when you leave a room (but not when your little brother is taking a bath!).

Ask if you can swap out ordinary light bulbs for the energy-saving kind.

Ask if you can set your refrigerator to about 40 degrees to save energy usage.

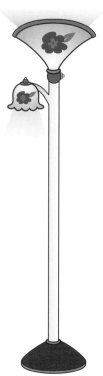

Do you have items around your house that use power for no reason? Do you leave on your curling iron after you are finished with it? Is the TV blaring in the den even though you're now eating in the kitchen? Do you leave your computer on after you've gone to bed? Flip the switch and save some $$$!

Go around your house and carefully dust the light bulbs. Yes, everyone in the house will think you have lost your mind, but believe it or not, the dusty ones use more electricity.

Check the dryer when clothes are drying. They might be dry before the timer buzzes. Or if you are really getting into this money-saving thing, hang your wet clothes outside and let God provide a free dryer!

TAKIN' CARE OF BUSINESS
Honesty Still Pays
(Based on Proverbs 22:16)

Jillian opened the envelope and shouted, "Yes! I get to go to Camp Yahweh this summer!"

The letter was from a local community organization where Jillian had applied for a scholarship to help pay her camp fees. To Jillian's surprise, the letter said they would pay her fees completely. She could go to camp for free!

Later that evening while Jillian was reviewing the scholarship information again, she saw that in order to receive help she had to have lived in the area for at least a year. But Jillian's family had just moved there nine months earlier!

Oh, no, Jillian thought. She wondered if she should tell anyone. After all, the organization would never know. Jillian wrestled in her sleep that night as she worried about the right thing to do.

That morning, Jillian told her problem to her best friend, Angie. "Don't worry. No one will ever know," Angie said with a wink.

Then Brittany, who overheard the conversation, chimed in with "Yeah, everybody lies. It's no big deal."

But Jillian felt she needed to be honest. So she prayed, "Oh, God, please help me. I really wanted to go to this camp, but I know I have to be honest."

That afternoon, Jillian told her mom what happened and ask her to drive her to the organization's office. She wanted to let them know that they should give the scholarship to someone else.

Jillian approached the office and waved at the man standing on the other side of the window.

"Hello, may I help you?" he asked.

"Yes, I can't accept your scholarship for camp this year," Jillian said with tears in her eyes. "I have to be honest. God wants me to be that way." She went on to explain how she had misread the instructions and realized she didn't qualify for the scholarship.

The man listened, then said, "One moment, please." He walked over to a desk and made a phone call. He returned smiling.

Nifty Thrifty Tip

Ask your mom and dad to let you do the grocery shopping for one meal. Have them give you a budget for what it usually costs to make dinner for your family. Try to stay within the budget and not go over. Next time, try to do it for even less!

"Jillian, I appreciate your honesty. And, because of it, we want to still pay for your camp – it's on the house!" the man grinned.

"Oh, thank you," Jillian said joyfully. She ran to tell her mother standing outside the door.

"Mom, you're right. Honesty does still pay!" she said as she threw her arms around her mom's neck.

God wants you to be honest. The wisest and richest man in the Bible, Solomon, said, "He who oppresses the poor to increase his wealth and he who gives gifts to the rich – both come to poverty." Be truthful and honest with people. That's how you would want them to treat you!

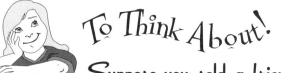

To Think About!

Suppose you sold a friend something and she paid you too much for it by mistake. Would you return the extra? Why or why not?

Prayer

Dear God, thank You for helping me find ways to save money and put it to better use. Help me to be honest with the money I have. In Jesus' name, amen.

Green Back FACT

"Time is money."

Whoever came up with that saying knew what he or she was talking about. When you give of yourself and your time, you are really giving someone something costly!

$ CHAPTER FOUR $

GIVE IT AWAY

Let's pretend you receive directions and a map to a place called Financial Freedom. You follow the directions exactly (yes, you are able to drive in this fantasy!), except you miss one road sign (because you were too busy fooling with the radio dial!). Anyway, the sign was one of those yellow, diamond-shaped ones with a wiggly arrow. It says "Generosity."

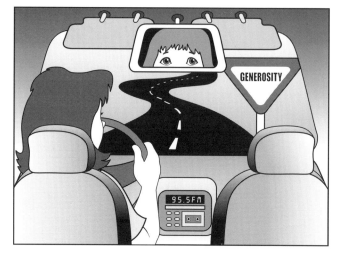

Well, you think, what's the big deal anyway? After all, yellow usually means caution so it's not like you have to obey it. It's only a suggestion.

Before you know it, the road starts curving around a sharp corner, then quickly weaves back the other way. Your hands tighten around your wallet...uh, the steering wheel.

"Yikes, this is scary!" you say nervously. "I was supposed to get off this road. Did I miss a turn? This isn't on the map. What is going on?"

Nifty Thrifty Tip

Get creative! Make your own gift wrap using poster paper, markers, glitter, rubber stamps and paints.

Lots of Christians have gone down this road, financially speaking. They don't pay attention to the directions God gives them in the Bible about financial freedom and prosperity. They miss the most important road sign while they are traveling down the road of life – maybe because it is a yellow one and not a red one. God *wants* everyone to be generous toward Him and each other, but that doesn't mean we *will*. He wants us to do it out of a good heart.

But if you choose to go against God and hold onto all of your money, you should get ready for a bumpy, curvy ride. There are going to be all kinds of things jumping out in front of you: plasma TVs, digital cameras, color cell phones. They will be like deer leaping and jackrabbits hopping across your path! And the farther down the road you go, the harder it will be to find your way back.

God's caution sign – "generosity" – warns believers about greed and helps keep things in perspective. It is not about what you can do for others, but rather what giving will do for you! It deepens your faith. It is an active choice to stay involved in the lives of others. You might find that giving brings more satisfaction than buying something for yourself. So get back on the right road. Give!

☀OFFER IT UP☀

A portion of all the money you earn belongs to God. Most Christians figure this "tithe" by giving one-tenth of their income to the work of the church. When you tithe, you are following God's command to give back to Him, and He will bless you for doing it (see Malachi 3:11). As you read the Bible, you will find many  examples of people who gave generously and were then blessed by God in ways they did not think were possible.

Tithing is all about giving back to God, but money is not the only way you can tithe. Offering "free" services also can be your tithe. For example, if your neighbor needs a babysitter so she can go to Bible study, you can offer to help her at no pay – and count that time as a tithe. Whether you give time or money, your life will be blessed for it.

☀FOR RICHER OR FOR POORER☀

Yes, tithing results in blessings. But let's get something straight: the more you give to God does not necessarily mean He will give you more *money* in return. Have you ever heard that it's better to give a gift than to receive one? That's because God made us to love others. He blesses us with joy when we give to others. And blessings of joy are way more valuable than money. Joy can't be bought!

God blesses in all sorts of ways. In Bible times, for example, God blessed Abraham and Lot with great wealth. But others were blessed with happy families, good health and lives of contentment. Even Job, who lost everything, was blessed because he never lost his faith in God. With what do you think God will bless you when you tithe for His work? Try it and find out!

Good Cents Scripture

Give, and it will be given to you. A good measure, pressed down, shaken together and running over, will be poured into your lap.

~ Luke 6:38

☀MAKE ME AN OFFERING☀

Sometimes you might have some extra money that you want to give to God, too. These "offerings" are above and beyond your tithe. For example, you could make an offering to help missionaries or to help a family in your church.

Be sure to always make your offering with a cheerful heart, not grudgingly. The Bible says in 2 Corinthians 9:7-8, "Each man [person] should give what he has decided in his heart to give, not reluctantly or under compulsion, for God loves a cheerful giver. And God is able to make all grace abound to you, so that in all things at all times, having all that you need, you will abound in every good work." God promises that when you give willingly, He will always provide for you.

Dear Miss Pursestrings,

The girl next door asked me if I could help out with a fund raiser for the Crisis Pregnancy Center. I really love doing community service and I especially love babies, so I really want to do this. But this girl is kind of weird and not popular at all. If my friends at school see me hanging out with her, they won't think I am cool anymore. What should I do?

Sincerely,
Wanna B. Popular

Dear Wanna,

It's really great that you want to help such a worthwhile cause. It sounds like you have the ministry of helping, which is a gift from God. Bravo! God will reward your obedience when you do what He has called you to do. Don't let your other friends control you. You'll miss out on God's call on your life! If they choose not to be your friends anymore, they probably weren't great friends to begin with. And, who knows, your neighbor might turn out to be really cool anyway!

Miss Pursestrings

Dear Miss Pursestrings,

At church I've heard the pastor talk about giving your way out of debt. How is that possible? I mean, the more you give, the less money you have. Right?

Sincerely,
Tina Tightwad

Dear Tina,

It's one of the mysteries of God – a secret hidden from those who don't know Him: The more freely you give, the less you will be entangled with the greed weed. God's Word says that when we give to others, we are actually lending to Him (Proverbs 19:17). He promises to repay you with much more than you give! You probably won't see money falling from the sky into your front yard, but God will repay you in other ways, such as joy and contentment. And He will have a treasure chest of riches waiting for you in heaven. God wants you to be a blessing to those in need.

Miss Pursestrings

☀WHEN TO GIVE☀

Many Christians tithe each week at church. Others tithe as soon as they get paid. The best way to ensure you don't spend the money you want to tithe is to set it aside in your "God's Work" envelope as soon as you get paid. Then when you are ready, you can take it with you to church. If you are sending the money to a charity, ask your mom or dad to write a check – never send cash in the mail.

GOD'S WORK

Soon you will be experiencing joy in knowing that you are helping someone else!

WHY DO YOU GIVE?*

Read each question and choose the answer that best describes you. Find out why you give by grading yourself at the end.

1. Your church is raising funds for a new building. When the offering basket is passed to you, you…

A. Throw in a dollar because you know your friends are watching.

B. Drop in some change because you figure you won't miss it.

C. Put in as much as you can because you want to help build God's kingdom.

2. You see a homeless person on the sidewalk, begging for work. You give him a dollar as you walk by. When your friends ask you why, you…

A. Say you felt sorry for him.

B. Tell them you had an extra dollar in your pocket.

C. Explain to them that you want him to see the love of God through you.

3. You are standing in line at the grocery store, and the person in front of you is short 50 cents. You…

A. Feel embarrassed for her so you turn your head.

B. Know you have plenty of money to spare, so you hand the clerk the change.

C. Quickly fish 50 cents out of your pocket, because God wants us to share.

4. Your friends are volunteering at the local rescue mission. You…

A. Volunteer, even though you really don't want to.

B. Volunteer because you have nothing better to do on Saturdays.

C. Volunteer because you want to tell the people about Jesus.

5. A lady from church asks you to babysit, but you heard your parents talking about her family's financial problems. You…

A. Babysit for free because you feel bad about charging her.

B. Babysit for free because you just got $20 on your birthday anyway.

C. Babysit for free, because it's what Jesus would do.

Mostly A's: Out of Guilt

Beware! You give because of the way you feel. Instead, give because God loves a cheerful giver.

Mostly B's: Chump Change

Uh, oh! You give because you won't lose anything by it. And, besides, it cleans out your pocket. Watch out, God says He would rather us be hot or cold. Love Him or hate Him. Be for Him or against Him, but not lukewarm.

Mostly C's: Love of God

Bravo! You give to show people your love for God.

DO U LUV MONEY?

Fill in the blanks of this sentence to discover a wise Scripture about money. You will use one of the words twice.

money**wealth****satisfied****income**

"Whoever loves _____ never has _____ enough; whoever

loves _____ is never _____ with his _____ ."

~ **Ecclesiastes 5:10**

☀GIVING PROJECT☀

Raising money for a local homeless shelter or another local charity makes good cents! Here's how:

1. Ask your parents or teachers which local organization they think will benefit the most.

2. Find out more about the group by checking the Internet or researching at the library.

3. Tell all your friends and neighbors. Try to recruit others to join you in your efforts.

4. Choose a fun theme, such as a 60's music dance-a-thon (borrow music from mom or dad).

5. Make posters and hang them in nearby locations so others will know the date, time and cost.

6. Create a pledge form for dancers to recruit sponsors. Be sure to include space for the sponsors' names, phone numbers and how much they pledge for each hour danced.

7. Have the dancers find sponsors who will pay a certain amount for each hour they dance. At the end of the dance-a-thon, log the number of hours each person danced.

8. Each dancer will be responsible for collecting the funds and giving them to you. Have fun!

❋DONATIONS❋

Do you have stuff just lying around collecting dust? Put it to good use and give it a second chance at the thrift shop. Mom and Dad can write off the donation on their taxes.

TAKIN' CARE OF BUSINESS
A Love Offering
(Based on Mark 12:41-44)

At the Biltmore Baptist Church, Sunday school teacher Mrs. Jones brought out the basket used for tithes and offerings. She placed it on a table and said, "Okay, kids, it's time to bring our tithes to God. After you do, please return to your seats. Then we will read a story from the Bible."

The Nelson twins dropped in their usual $2 each. Jack jingled his envelope of change before tossing in the coins. Tom, a rich kid from the west side of town, waved around his $10 bill like a flag before dropping in into the basket.

After everyone had returned to their seats, the door opened. They all turned to see who was coming in. Amy shyly entered the room. She was wearing a badly worn dress and mismatched socks. Her hair was flat and a bit messy, but her face lit up when she saw Mrs. Jones.

Nifty Thrifty Tip

Get your hair cut at a beauty school. Their services are much cheaper than salons, and you'll probably get an even more stylish cut!

"I'm so glad you could make it, Amy." Mrs. Jones greeted her. "We were just giving our tithes and offerings."

"Oh, good!" Amy said happily. "I brought all my money to give to God."

Amy dropped two quarters into the basket, then she sat down.

"God is pleased that you want to give all that you have," Mrs. Jones said as she smiled at Amy.

The other kids snickered at Amy's offering.

"What's so great about two quarters?" Tom sneered. "I gave God 10 whole dollars."

"Well, Tom, that's nice that you gave God a lot of money," said Mrs. Jones, "but we have to be sure our motives are right and that we are doing it for the right reason. We give because we love Jesus, not because we want others to think we are important or better than them."

Mrs. Jones walked over to where Amy was sitting and put a gentle hand on her shoulder. "Even though Amy has given a small amount of money, she gave all that she had. God loves when we are willing to give everything to Him."

Mrs. Jones looked down and saw Amy with a broad smile across her face.

To Think About!

Have you ever given "for show" in a way that wasn't from your heart or for the right reasons? What happened?

Prayer

Dear God, please help me always to give with a cheerful and pure heart. In Jesus' name, amen.

Green Back FACT

Where is Wall Street? It's an actual street in New York City where many people work in the money business. The most famous place on Wall Street is the New York Stock Exchange (NYSE). You might have seen the close of the NYSE on TV, when a bell rings as a group of people cheer for the day's good numbers. These are people who invest their money in companies by buying shares. A share is a very small piece of the company – the more shares you own, the bigger your piece of the company. The price of a share goes up and down depending on how well a company is doing. The object is to buy a share when it is low and sell when the share is high, so you can make a profit!

$ CHAPTER FIVE $

A PENNY SAVED

It's fun to spend money, but if you want to buy something that costs more than what you have, you will need to save for it. Having a "nest egg" – that's a funny way to say "savings" – allows you to make larger purchases. It also gives you money to fall back on in case of an emergency. Your parents probably have a nest egg or two right now, such as a savings account for your college tuition.

☀ GO FOR THE GOAL ☀

Your envelopes (or jars) are a great way to save for short-term goals, such as inexpensive items or activities in the near future. But if you earn more money than you need to spend right away, you will want to keep it in a safer place. Banks are the best choice for your long-term savings.

There are three reasons why you can bank on banks to keep your money safe and sound:

1 Banks are insured by the government. So even if your bank is robbed or goes out of business, you will get your money back (up to $100,000!).

2 Banks actually pay you to give them your money! The more money you put in the bank, the more "interest" – that's money! – you will earn. This interest is like a thank-you for letting them use your money.

3 If your money is in a bank – instead of in your pocket or desk drawer – you are less likely to spend it. The extra effort it takes for you to get to the bank might make you think twice before you drop $5 on that new nail polish!

If you think banks are just for adults, think again. Most banks have special programs just for kids. Talk with your parents about opening a bank account, then check some local banks for options. Most banks have "student accounts" that are easy to open and charge low or no fees.

Good Cents Scripture

Do not store up for yourselves treasures on earth, where moth and rust destroy, and where thieves break in and steal.

~ Matthew 6:19

Dear Miss Pursestrings,

I've heard the saying "save for a rainy day." What does rain have to do with saving money?

Sincerely,
Sunny Davis

Dear Sunny,

The saying "save for a rainy day" means to save for a time you might need it. This expression has been around since the 16th century. Back then, rain meant there could be a leaky roof, or no work for farmers. So people needed to have extra money saved for their time  of need. Today, it's still a good idea to have an "emergency" fund for the unexpected. For instance, if you start a business delivering newspapers and your bike tire has a flat – you'll need a few dollars quickly to get a new tube. All budgets should include a rainy day fund.

Miss Pursestrings

Dear Miss Pursestrings,

I have a serious problem with saving. I just love bargains and digging in bins of clearance items. I always can find the best deals. But now I want to buy something that costs more than I have. My mom said, "If you want something, you are going to have to save for it." So how does someone like me reach her goal, if she has never saved a dime?

Sincerely,
Notta Saver

Dear Notta,

Don't be too hard on yourself. There are plenty of people who struggle with saving. If money seems to burn a hole in your pocket, then make sure you first set aside portions for tithes and savings as soon as you get some money. Then only carry with you the amount you can spend. It is a lot easier to control your spending when you limit how much you have in your wallet. Eventually, you will have enough to get the item you wanted.

Miss Pursestrings

Make It!

MISS PIGGY BANK

Here's a really cute papier-mâché bank for stashing your cash – and it will last a long time! This project will take a few days for the layers to dry. It's messy, so wear old clothing and cover the area you are working on with newspaper. Check out the next page for what you need, then follow the directions to first make the glue, and then make the bank.

What You Need

flour

cool water

boiling water

cardboard

measuring cups

sauce pan

old newspapers

1 balloon

1 pink chenille wire

knife (ask an adult to help you cut hole)

black marker

masking tape

pink tissue paper

1 paper egg carton (or cut 2 empty toilet rolls into sections)

cardboard

plastic wiggle eyes (optional)

pencil

What to Do

To make the glue:

1. Mix 1 cup of flour into 1 cup of water. The mixture will be thin and runny.

2. Ask an adult to heat 4 cups of water to a boil. Add the flour mixture to the hot water.

3. Simmer for 3 minutes, then cool.

To make the Miss Piggy Bank:

1. While the glue is cooling, blow up a balloon and tie it in a knot. This will be Miss Piggy Bank's body.

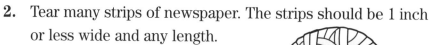

2. Tear many strips of newspaper. The strips should be 1 inch or less wide and any length.

3. Dip each strip into the cooled glue. Then starting anywhere, wrap it around the balloon.

4. Cover the pig's body with two or three layers. Let each layer dry before adding the next layer. After the pig is completely covered, let it dry overnight.

5. To add legs and a snout, separate five paper egg carton sections. Tape one section over the knotted end of the balloon for the snout. Attach four more to the bottom of the oval-shape for its legs.

6. To add ears, cut diamond shapes from cardboard and bend the shapes in half. Attach the folded halves to her head using masking tape.

7. To add color, first tear tissue paper into small pieces (about 2 inches square). Cover the pig with a thin layer of glue using your fingers. Then attach the tissue pieces on your pig. Occasionally add more glue until it's nicely coated.

8. Let Miss Piggy Bank dry overnight.

9. Ask an adult to poke a small hole in the pig's tail end for inserting the chenille wire.

10. Tightly wrap a pink pipe cleaner around a pencil to create a curly tail. Slide it off the pencil. Gently pull out one end and insert the end into the tail hole.

11. Use a black marker to draw eyes, or glue on wiggle eyes.

12. Draw two nostrils for her snout.

13. Ask an adult to cut a slot along the top of the pig's body that is large enough to fit any coin.

Optional: You may want to add a coat of varnish for shine and protection, but ask an adult to help first.

☀YOU CAN ACCOUNT ON THESE☀

There are two main kinds of bank accounts: checking and savings. A checking account is used mostly to spend money. Except for an account with a very high balance (the total money in the account), a checking account does not pay interest. So whatever money you put in a checking account is all you will have. Also, a checking account makes it really easy for you to use your money by providing checks and ATM cards. It can be difficult to keep track of a checking account because of the constant flow of money in and out of the account. Many banks won't open checking accounts for kids because of this responsibility. For all these reasons, you probably do not want to get a checking account to help you save money.

If you want to see your money grow – and you don't plan to take out ("withdraw") money too often – a savings account is your best choice.

Nifty Thrifty Tip

Bring your lunch to school instead of buying it in the cafeteria. Save your "dough" for something you'll "knead" later.

Savings accounts pay you interest on your money. But they also charge fees if you make too many withdrawals. So be sure and keep some money at home to meet your short-term goals.

When you open your account, the bank will give you

withdrawal and deposit slips that have your name and account number on them. You will use these each time you visit your bank and want to put in or take out money from your account. When you take your slip to the teller, he or she will process your transaction and give you a receipt as proof of your deposit.

In addition to getting withdrawal and deposit slips when you open your account, you also will receive a little book to keep track of them. This is called a "register." Be sure to always write your deposits and withdrawals in your register. Ask your mom or dad to help you get the hang of it at first.

When you open your savings account, the bank might give you an ATM (Automated Teller Machine) card to go with it. ATM cards are fun to have because you can make deposits and withdrawals when you want – even when the bank is closed. But beware: the easier you can get at your money, the more likely you will be to spend it. If you are truly serious about saving, ask the bank not to issue an ATM card with your account. Or if you do receive one, give it to your parents to keep in a safe place for you.

You will earn interest on your savings account four times per year. The bank will send you a statement that shows how much interest you earned. Write this amount in your register as a deposit!

Most banks now have online services where you can go onto their Web sites and check your account's balance, withdrawals and deposits. It's a great way to keep an eye on things. Go on your bank's Web site for more details on getting started.

☀DEALING WITH CARDS☀

Credit cards are plastic cards that look like ATM cards, but they have been around a lot longer than ATM cards. Credit cards are a convenient way to buy things – "charge" them to an account – so you don't have to carry cash or checks, and some can even be

used in ATM machines to borrow cash from the bank. Of course, all of this charging is a loan – eventually, you have to pay back everything you put on your credit card. And when you don't, the bank charges you interest (instead of paying you like it does for your savings account!). Every month that you don't pay the full amount, the bank charges you more and more interest. You can end up paying more in fees than the item cost!

Because of this interest, credit cards are dangerous for some people. The cards seem to provide "free" money, which makes it too easy to spend money you can't pay back. The best rule for credit cards is to pay them off every month. At the very least you should have a plan to pay back the loan within a short period of time. Otherwise, you can get into terrible debt.

Good Cents
Scripture

Let no debt remain outstanding, except the continuing debt to love one another.

~ Romans 13:8

Gift cards are a great alternative to credit cards, especially for kids. Most department stores, specialty stores and grocery stores have these reloadable cards. You can buy them in set values – such as $10, $20, $50 or $100. After you use up the money on the card, you can reload it with more money. So you get the benefit of credit cards – not having to carry cash – without the pitfalls of spending more than you have. Plus, anyone can buy and use a gift card, no matter what age!

✳ MONEY ADDS UP ✳

Check out these tips for savvy saving.

Put a small jar or container in your room. When you have extra coins, throw them in the jar. A few coins here and there really add up!

Before starting to save, get advice from your parents or a pastor about your plans. They will help you figure out your goals and how to achieve them.

Once you build a good amount of money, move it from your envelopes to a savings account where it can earn interest in a safe place.

Speed up your savings by cutting back on some spending, such as buying candy after school. Stow this extra change with the rest of your savings and you will reach your goals more quickly.

Make your dreams a reality! Set a date for when you will accomplish each goal.

Ask family members to give you cash instead of gifts for holidays and birthdays. Add this money to your savings.

When you set goals, figure out a way to measure them. For example, have a goal for getting three babysitting jobs each week, or try to save $50 a month.

Stay flexible. You may need to make adjustments to how much you set aside each week, or change deadlines along the way.

Write your goals in your calendar or on a piece of paper where you will see them each day.

See yourself reaching your goal. Get a picture of those in-line skates you're saving for and look at it every time you feel the urge to blow your savings.

☀BARTERING☀

Bartering is exchanging a service or product for something you want. You've probably read about early Americans who bartered. Indians traded animal skins and corn for guns and spices from the settlers. But bartering is still a good way to get what you need today. You might not be looking for animal skins, but your friend's tennis racket might be worth your skates. Just be sure you check with your parents first before bartering.

QUICK QUIZ — SAV-O-METER☀

Are you a saver or a hoarder? Find out by circling the letter that best describes you.

1. Friends frequently tell you...

A. "You really know how to find a bargain."

B. "You're a tightwad."

2. When you join a club, you...

A. immediately run for treasurer.

B. avoid paying your dues as long as possible.

3. When your relatives visit, your parents tell them...

A. "She should be an accountant when she grows up."

B. "She takes after Uncle Nick – he stashed away every dime."

4. When your teacher asks your class where you would like to go on a field trip, you suggest…

A. the mall.

B. canceling the trip and refunding everyone's money.

5. When a classmate says she forgot her lunch money, you…

A. agree to loan her the money if she'll pay you back tomorrow.

B. sink down in your chair, hoping she won't ask you for a loan.

6. A great gift for you would be…

A. a change sorter.

B. a miniature safe with a combination lock.

7. Which person best describes you?

A. George Bailey from "It's a Wonderful Life."

B. Ebenezer Scrooge from "A Christmas Carol."

8. Which section of the newspaper do you look at first?

A. The ads, then the comics.

B. The business section, then you throw it in the recycling bin.

9. Which TV channel are you most likely to watch?

A. The Do-It-Yourself Channel

B. CNBC – or nothing at all

10. You spend your free time by…

A. Writing your dreams and goals for your future in your journal.

B. Counting all your loot.

Turn the page for your results…

Mostly A's?

You're a smart penny pincher who knows how to save and be resourceful. Your good cents will add up, so be sure and splurge on yourself every now and then.

Mostly B's?

You've got the tight-fisted saving thing down pat. It may be wise to consider making some goals, instead of just saving to save. Look for ways to give and share what you have with others.

Good Cents Scripture

Remember this: Whoever sows sparingly will also reap sparingly, and whoever sows generously will also reap generously.

~ 2 Corinthians 9:6

TAKIN' CARE OF BUSINESS
The Generous Woman
(Based on 1 Kings 17:8-16)

Bang! Bang! Bang!

What now? thought the poor woman when she heard the pounding at her door. She smoothed a blanket over her weak, starving son and hurried to the door.

Flinging it open, she was surprised to see a good-looking man in an expensive suit with a big smile on his face. He seemed to glow!

"Hello, my name is Ken Price and I have a special for you today," he said smoothly. "For just three easy payments of $29.99, you can own this lovely 24-piece china set! All major credit cards accepted."

"I'm sorry, Mr. Price," the woman sighed. "But I don't have any money. In fact, my son and I were just about to eat our last meal together before we run out of food completely. This drought has been terrible."

But Ken didn't seem to hear what she said. "You know, this door-to-door business of mine has made me hungry," he said. "Could you make me a sandwich?"

"But I only have enough for me and my son."

"Just make the sandwich."

While Ken made himself at home, the woman put her last two slices of bread on a plate. She scraped the last bits of peanut butter from the jar and spread it on one slice. On the other, she squeezed her last drops of grape jelly. She gave the sandwich to Ken and watched him eat it.

"Yum! This is delicious. Thank you," he said, wiping a smudge of peanut butter from his mouth.

"I am glad you liked it," the woman said as she looked with worry toward the bedroom door where her son was sleeping.

"Don't worry," Ken said. "Because you were generous and you gave me your last meal, God will bless you and take care of you."

Nifty Thrifty Tip

Avoid pricey vending machines. Make your own "snack packs" by filling sandwich bags with chips, cookies and other snacks.

The poor woman took the empty plate to the kitchen. Looking inside the dark pantry, she was shocked to find a whole loaf of bread, a full jar of peanut butter and a container of grape jelly hidden in the back.

"Thanks be to God!" she shouted. "Now my son and I can live!"

The bread, peanut butter and jelly in the old lady's pantry lasted until the end of the drought.

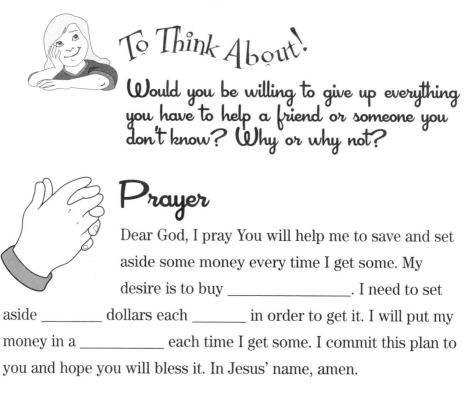

To Think About!

Would you be willing to give up everything you have to help a friend or someone you don't know? Why or why not?

Prayer

Dear God, I pray You will help me to save and set aside some money every time I get some. My desire is to buy _____. I need to set aside _____ dollars each _____ in order to get it. I will put my money in a _____ each time I get some. I commit this plan to you and hope you will bless it. In Jesus' name, amen.

Green Back FACT

Did you know that coins are made like cookies? Okay, not exactly. But coinmakers do heat sheets of metal and press them into thin sheets. Then they cut the blank metal into coin shapes. The coins are then heated and cleaned, and finally stamped. American pennies are made from copper-coated zinc, while nickels are made from a combination of copper and nickel. Dimes, quarters and half-dollars are made with layers of copper and nickel pressed together. So coins may be baked, but they are for buying, not biting!

CHAPTER SIX

SPEND SOME!

Spending money can be one of the most enjoyable benefits of earning it! You can use it for things you need and want. And your budget will keep you on track so you don't use up all of your money accidentally.

☀Needs VS. WANTS☀

It is important to figure out your needs (what you must have) and wants (what would like to have but could live without). Having money for school lunches or class supplies are needs, while going to the movies or buying DVDs are wants. To help you decide, make a list of the costs of your needs and wants below. Then fill in the equations at the bottom to figure out what you have leftover.

Needs	Wants	Tithes & Savings
_____	_____	_____
_____	_____	_____
_____	_____	_____
_____	_____	_____
Total: _____	Total: _____	Total: _____

Needs _____ + Tithes & Savings _____ = Must Have _____

Income: _____ - Must Have _____ = Leftover _____

What is leftover is what you have to use on your Wants. If you aren't happy with your total for Wants, you need to adjust your Needs list. For example, could you bring a sack lunch instead of buying your lunch? Could you share with a friend instead of buying all new supplies for Art Club? Also, make sure before spending any money that you take care of business: God first, then savings, and pay back any loans or overdue fines you might have. Now, the rest is yours. Make it last by not blowing it all in one day!

Good Cents Scripture

Jesus looked at him and said, "How hard it is for the rich to enter the kingdom of God! Indeed, it is easier for a camel to go through the eye of a needle than for a rich man to enter the kingdom of God."

~ Luke 18:24-25

Dear Miss Pursestrings,

I have a friend who buys anything she wants. Her mom even gave her a credit card to use whenever she feels like it. She shops at the most expensive clothing stores at the mall. She is so spoiled – it makes me sick! I would have to save up my allowances for three whole months just to buy one shirt like hers. What should I do?

Sincerely,
Penny Less

Dear Penny,

Sometimes it can be hard to be content with your situation in life, especially when you see others getting what you want. Try not to worry about what your friend is getting and keep your eyes on God instead. Make a list of all the things He has given you, and you will be surprised! Thank Him for the things you do have and remember He will provide for all of your needs.

Miss Pursestrings

Dear Miss Pursestrings,

I bought an electronic diary, but now it doesn't work. I've only had it a week. I want to take it back to the store, but I have never done that and I'm scared. What do I do?

Sincerely,
Mia Shopper

Dear Mia,

It's disappointing when you buy something and it breaks right away. But many items are covered by a warranty, which means the manufacturer will fix your diary free of charge. Check the box to see if your diary has a warranty. If not, return it to the store where you bought it (take the receipt with you). Explain the problem and the clerk probably will exchange it for a new one, give you a refund or give you a store credit (so you can buy something else).

Miss Pursestrings

Dear Miss Pursestrings,

I saw an ad on TV for glitter jeans and now everyone at school has a pair. I begged and begged, but my mom says she isn't going to spend $65 on a pair of decorated jeans when I can get some plain ones for $20. But I want the real thing!

Sincerely,
Jean Needer

Dear Jean,

Ads will try to get you to buy things you can't afford or don't need. We are bombarded every day by commercials and ads trying to convince us to buy products. Some will try to tell you that everyone has it, so you must get it, too. Some will use your favorite TV or

sports star to make you think it must be really good. But remember, celebrities get paid to promote products. Maybe they don't even like that perfume or those tennis shoes! So try to understand what your mom is saying. She is being practical and living within her budget. This is just a craze that will soon pass, and everyone will be on to something else. But for now, see if you can convince your mom to buy some spray-on glitter from the craft store so you can make your regular jeans shimmer.

Miss Pursestrings

☀GOOD BUYING☀

Here are some tips and questions to ask yourself so you can be a smart shopper.

Is there a less expensive version of the same product? A cheaper brand is often just as good as the name brand.

Ask yourself, "Do I really need it? Does it go with pants or a skirt I already have? Can I wear it to school and church?"

Is this the best price you have seen for this item? Have you shopped around to make sure?

Check with your parents to see if they think it's wise to buy this item now. If it will require more money for maintenance, you may want to wait until you can really afford it.

If this is a big purchase, have you researched it carefully? Find out as much as you can about the product. Check the Internet or read about it at the library.

Is this the best time to make your purchase? Is it just before Christmas, or a family member's birthday, when you will need the money for other things?

Does the item reflect your beliefs and testimony for Jesus? Is it something you would hide in embarrassment when church friends are over?

Do you have a good feeling about buying it? Is there a major disadvantage to making this purchase?

Look for bargains at thrift and second-hand shops. Items that are slightly used may save you lots of money.

MUG SHOTS

Which President belongs on which bill? Draw a line from a face to its matching bill.

Answers: George Washington on the $1 bill, Thomas Jefferson on the $2 bill, Abraham Lincoln on the $5 bill, Alexander Hamilton on the $10 bill, Andrew Jackson on the $20 bill, Ulysses S. Grant on the $50 bill, and Benjamin Franklin on the $100 bill.

❊SMART SHOPPER❊

Being thrifty is one of the best ways to stretch a dollar. It can really make a difference to buy wisely.

No matter where you shop – department stores, supercenters, boutiques or the Internet – you will want to get the most bang for your buck. Comparison shopping is one way to be sure you get it! Compare these five things when hunting for the best buy:

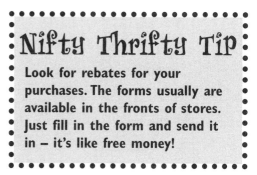

PRICE

How much an item costs is probably the most important thing to consider. Typically, name brands cost more than generic off brands because of advertising and promotion. In many cases, they are just as good. Ask yourself, "Do I need to have the name brand that will cost me more, or will the cheaper off-brand do?"

SIZE

Packaging plays a major role in what gets our attention in stores, but don't let the size of the box fool you. It's what is inside that counts. Check the package for the size of

> ### Nifty Thrifty Tip
> Look for rebates for your purchases. The forms usually are available in the fronts of stores. Just fill in the form and send it in – it's like free money!

the contents, which is usually labeled in ounces and weight.

VALUE

Go for quantity over design. If the bundle of plain notepads costs the same as the rainbow-colored ones – but you get eight plain vs.

six rainbow in a package – go for the plain ones. After all, they will still do the job!

QUALITY

Check each product to see if it is made well. It can be worth the extra money to get a product that is made better and therefore will last longer.

PREMIUMS

This little gimmick can blind you to the actual value of the item. Does the toy in the cereal box really make the cereal worth an extra dollar? On the other hand, the lip gloss that comes with a free nail polish is probably worth the extra 50 cents.

When you compare price, size, value, quality and premiums, you won't only save a lot of money – you'll be left with money for a special treat after a hard day of shopping!

 # DEEP SEA SPENDING ☀

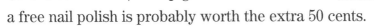

Are you a savvy spender or do you spend every last dime you have? Find out if your spending habits are wise or foolish by circling the answer below that best describes you.

1. Which sweatshirt would you buy?

 A. A name-brand sweatshirt in your favorite color.

 B. A cheaper version that looks identical so you have money left for earrings.

2. When a blockbuster movie hits the theaters, you…

 A. raid your piggy bank so you can buy popcorn, soda and candy to enjoy every minute of it.

 B. eat at home before you go so you won't blow your budget.

3. When you see the summer's hottest bathing suits advertised on TV, you…

A. beg your mom to take you to the store right away.

B. wait a few weeks and watch the ads for sales.

4. Packs of pencils are two for a dollar. You…

A. buy two even though one is plenty.

B. buy one pack.

5. Your best friend comes over wearing the latest designer watch. You…

A. immediately run out to buy one just like it.

B. compliment her, then show her the Mickey Mouse watch you got from Disney World a few years ago.

6. When you go to the ice cream parlor, you…

A. order the triple scoop sundae because it's on sale, even though it's more than you can eat.

B. order your usual one scoop of chocolate.

7. While shopping at a bookstore, you spot your favorite science fiction series. You…

A. buy the whole series, even though you read the first two at the library.

B. buy one to take home and read before buying the next one.

8. You see a really cool video game advertised on TV. You…

A. grab your purse and run out to the store to get it.

B. wait a week to see if you really want it.

9. You decide to start your own jewelry-making business. You…

   A. dash off to the store to buy all the supplies and books you need.

   B. go online and do research for the best deals on supplies and books.

10. This spring you decide to start a garden. You…

   A. buy small plants from a home and garden center.

   B. buy seeds to start plants at home.

Mostly A's

Your spending ship is sailing in rough waters. Fishy advertisements are stealing your money off your hook. Try not to buy things you don't need; work on living on a budget and set goals. This will help you save up for big fish, like a new bike or a computer.

Mostly B's

Smooth sailing is ahead for your spending ship! You know when to cast out your money because you're reeling in big savings. Steer clear of advertisement hurricanes and only buy things you really need. Just don't forget to have a little fun every now and then and buy yourself a treat!

Green Back FACT

The entire nation of Israel was set free from debt in just one day! When a famine hit Israel, people had to borrow to be able have enough money to eat and pay their taxes. Times were so tough that some people even sold their children into slavery in order to survive! But all that changed in one day. Get your Bible and read about it in Nehemiah 5:1-13.

☀ THE PRICE IS RIGHT ☀

Sarah's mom has given her $100 to buy school clothes. She must buy two shirts and either a skirt or pants for her school uniform, but she can use the leftover money to buy any clothes she wants. Help Sarah to be a savvy shopper so she can get her school uniform and some other cool stuff to wear! Remember, she can't spend more than $100 (tax is included in these prices). Circle the pieces Sarah can buy with her budget.

❋AVOID SPENDING PITFALLS❋

Watch out for ad gimmicks that make products look bigger and better than they really are. Mail-order companies, catalogs and online services make shopping fun and easy, but be sure to read the ad carefully.

Read the small print before ordering. Check the description and note the size (dimensions), and other facts about the product. You might discover the backpack you're interested in is only three inches tall!

Be sure to add shipping and handling charges when shopping by mail or Internet. The final cost of the product may be more than buying it at a local store. But the flip side is you probably won't have to pay sales tax if you order from out-of-state.

Keep all paperwork you receive with the product in case you need to return it or have a question about your order.

Nifty Thrifty Tip

Closely inspect items before buying them. If something is flawed with a small stain or missing a button (and you think can fix it), ask for a discount.

Never send cash in the mail. Ask a parent to write a check or send a money order (you can get them at most convenience stores).

Don't ever feel pressure to buy. If you don't feel comfortable with your purchase, wait. Other bargains will come along.

SNAP DRAGONFLY MONEY CLIPS

Let these winged friends clip your money together!

What You Need

spring-type clothespins

acrylic paint, any color

two wiggle eyes per dragonfly
(buy at any craft store)

6-inch netting fabric

 ## What To Do

1. Paint your wooden clothespin any color you like. Allow to dry.

2. Glue the wiggle eyes near the bottom edge of the clothespin.

3. Fold the netting in half. Cut out two sets of wings along the fold as shown.

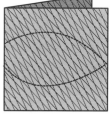

4. Pinch open the clothespin, dab a drop of glue on the wings and place them inside on the top of the clothespin.

5. Clip a piece of wax paper inside to prevent the wings from sticking together.

✳BATTLING BAD SPENDING HABITS✳

If you like to spend every dime or don't make wise decisions in your purchases, you're not alone. Some people just don't know how to say no. Or they haven't learned how to save and wait. Maybe you feel like you'd like to have everything. But where would you put it?

Nifty Thrifty Tip

Help others save! Adopt a family in need. Check with your church about how to help a family by doing odd jobs around the house with yard work, babysitting and so on.

Others may spend when they feel bad or are sad. They think buying something will make them feel better and bring joy. When they go home, they feel worse, because now they have no more money.

If any of these people sound like you, or you need help in another area, God is right there waiting for you to ask. With His help, you will be able to break these bad spending habits. All you have to do is put your heart and soul into it.

My bad spending/saving habits are:

_____

The one I would like to tackle first:

_____

I'm going to stop:

_____

I will do this by this date:

_____

How I will do this:

_____

Here's how I will reward myself:

_____

TAKIN' CARE OF BUSINESS
The Big Spender
(Based on Luke 15:11-24)

Once there was a teen boy named Josh who received $10 every week for his allowance. One day, he asked his dad to give him the whole $40 at once.

"Okay," Josh's dad said. "But that's it for this month." The boy grabbed the money and ran out the door.

"Yes!" he said. "Now I can have some fun."

So Josh bought a skateboard with glow-in-the-dark wheels, and a metallic silver helmet. He hung out at the skate park all day and made lots of friends.

"Hey, man," one guy yelled. "Could ya lend me some money?"

"No problem," Josh answered.

But it wasn't long before Josh ran out of money. To make matters worse, his new friends left him because it was getting near dinnertime.

When the skate park closed that evening, Josh stood there all alone. As he began to walk toward the bus stop to head for home, a gang jumped out from behind the bushes and stole his skateboard, helmet and the rest of his cash. Now he didn't even have money for the bus – and no skateboard!

Josh slowly walked home with his head hung low. *Man, I shouldn't have spent all of my money*, he thought. *Now I have nothing.*

Josh walked and walked until he was finally on his street. Looking up, he saw his father running down the street toward him. His dad grabbed him and gave him a bear hug.

"I was so worried!" his dad said. "It's nearly midnight. What happened?"

"I'm sorry, Dad," Josh cried. "I spent all of my money and lost everything."

"I'm sorry, too, Josh," his father replied. "But I forgive you, and God forgives you, too."

Have you ever blown it – whether it was money or sharing your Christian witness – and needed God's forgiveness? He is always ready and waiting to forgive you. All you have to do is ask – and promise to try better next time.

To Think About!

Have you ever sensed God leading you not to buy something, yet you did it anyway? How did it make you feel afterward?

Prayer

Dear God, please help me to make wise choices in my spending and investing. I want to be a good steward over all that You have given me. In Jesus' name, amen.

CHAPTER SEVEN

WORK IT, GIRLFRIEND!

As you get older, you'll want to have your own money

– which means you'll need to be responsible. You already may be earning an allowance by doing chores around the house. If so, your parents expect you to do what it takes to receive your allowance. Maybe you wash the dishes after dinner or you rake leaves in your yard or you walk and feed your dog. Whatever your chores are, you know if you don't do them you won't receive your allowance. But by keeping your word and doing the work, you get the money. That's showing you can handle responsibility!

If you are not working for an allowance, ask your parents how you can help around the house for extra money. Here are some chores you could offer to do, depending on whether you like working inside or outside (or both!):

Inside

Dust tables and shelves

Mop the floor

Vacuum the carpet

Set the table for meals

Clean the kitchen after meals

Do the laundry

Change the bed sheets

Clean the bathrooms

Babysit for younger brothers or sisters

Outside

Pull weeds

Rake leaves

Shovel walkways

Walk, feed or bathe pets

Take out the trash

☀SHOW ME THE MONEY!☀

If your parents don't want to give you an allowance – or you want more than they are willing to pay – you need to find other

Nifty Thrifty Tip

Don't know what to call your new business? Check out the Yellow Pages for ideas (just don't use any names already in the book!).

ways to make money. With a few exceptions, you can't get a regular paying job until you're 16. So until then, you'll need to think of some clever ways to turn on the cash flow.

The most important part of starting a business is making sure you truly like what you will be doing – because you will be doing a lot of it! If you don't like pulling weeds, for example, gardening is not going to be a good way for you to earn extra money. After a while, you'll dread going to work, then your business will fall off – and then you'll be back where you started: with no money!

QUICK QUIZ THE SKY IS THE LIMIT☀

Having trouble deciding the kind of business that might be right for you? Circle the picture below and on the next few pages that is before each activity you enjoy. Then count the pictures to see how to turn your faves into 5s…and 10s…and even 20s!

☀ **Playing with your Etch-a-Sketch.**™ ☆ **Reading books.**

🌙 **Thinking of ways to stop world hunger.** ☁ **Buying**

new in-line skates. 🌈 **Going to an outdoor concert.**

✈ **Feeding your neighbor's twins.** ☆ **Creating poetry.**

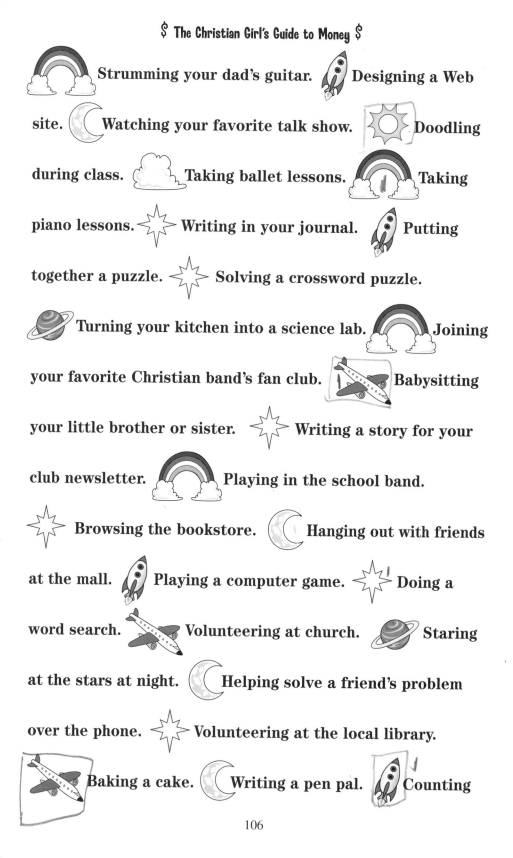

Strumming your dad's guitar. Designing a Web site. Watching your favorite talk show. Doodling during class. Taking ballet lessons. Taking piano lessons. Writing in your journal. Putting together a puzzle. Solving a crossword puzzle. Turning your kitchen into a science lab. Joining your favorite Christian band's fan club. Babysitting your little brother or sister. Writing a story for your club newsletter. Playing in the school band. Browsing the bookstore. Hanging out with friends at the mall. Playing a computer game. Doing a word search. Volunteering at church. Staring at the stars at night. Helping solve a friend's problem over the phone. Volunteering at the local library. Baking a cake. Writing a pen pal. Counting

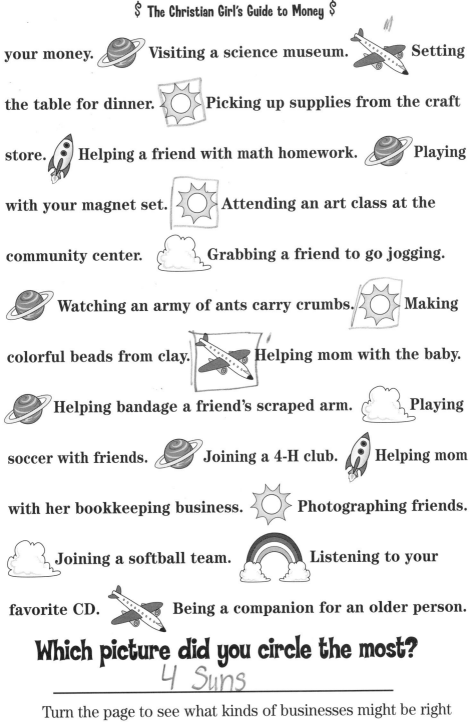

your money. Visiting a science museum. Setting the table for dinner. Picking up supplies from the craft store. Helping a friend with math homework. Playing with your magnet set. Attending an art class at the community center. Grabbing a friend to go jogging. Watching an army of ants carry crumbs. Making colorful beads from clay. Helping mom with the baby. Helping bandage a friend's scraped arm. Playing soccer with friends. Joining a 4-H club. Helping mom with her bookkeeping business. Photographing friends. Joining a softball team. Listening to your favorite CD. Being a companion for an older person.

Which picture did you circle the most?

4 Suns

Turn the page to see what kinds of businesses might be right for you. Then either follow the picture symbols or go straight to your chosen job (they are in alphabetical order) in Chapter 9 for all the how-to's on getting started in your new job!

Writing & Communication

* Curb Communicator
* Read 'Em Again Used Books
* Terrific Tutor
* That's News to Me!

Music & Entertainment

* Balloon Story Time Club
* Jamming DJ
* Music Teacher
* My Music Store

People & Animals

* The Cupid Connection
* Dog Walker
* House Sitting
* Mother's Helper
* Runaround You!

Sports & Recreation

* Ballpark Bites
* Flyer Distributor
* Movers-on-the-Go
* Summertime Sports Camp

Math & Computers

* Creative Cards
* Save-a-Lot Coupon Books
* Time-saving Typist
* Wide-Eyed Photography

Home Life

* Miss Clean
* Lip Smackin' Good Cookbook
* Dressing Designer
* Natural Cosmetics Company
* Party Planner

Arts & Crafts

* Coin Coasters
* Fancy Face Painter
* Gift Wrap Girl
* Personal Pets
* Pencil Power
* School Spirit Pennants

Science & Nature

* Garden Market
* Leaf It to Me Raking Service
* Lovely Lawns
* Pet Rocks
* Ready to Recycle
* Watch Your Money Grow Watering Can

Good Cents Scripture

Whatever you do, work at it with all your heart, as working for the Lord, not for men.
~ Colossians 3:23

☀MAKE A SCHEDULE☀

If you decide to start your own business, try not to get carried away with it and neglect your family, friends or homework! Keep your priorities in order by guarding your schedule. Remember, money and possessions are things you can always get, but time is something that can't be replaced. The Bible says in Ephesians 5:16 to "redeem the time," so be sure to make "the most" of the time you have been given.

Figure out if you have the time to do what you want to do. Grab a pencil (so you can erase and make changes later) and go to the Weekly Schedule Worksheet on page 188. Make a list of all the

things you do with your time, such as school, practices, homework, chores, family outings, church, etc. Write each one beside the hour you do them during a typical day. Don't forget to block out time for studying and sleeping!

Now look over your schedule. You may want to use a bright colored highlighter to color in blocks of time that could be used for your business. Count the hours you have highlighted to see if you have the time you need. Do you have time for an afternoon job? Or does a weekend-only job better suit you? Do you need a job that lets you set your own hours, such as making crafts? Or do you have enough time that you can work inside someone else's schedule, such as for babysitting? If you cannot answer yes to any of these, you may need to cut out an activity if you really want a job. Or plan to work just every now and then, such as running a yard sale or bake sale – one or two days of hard work…and it's over!

> ## Nifty Thrifty Tip
>
> Invest in your own business first by buying supplies you can use to make money.

Dear Miss Pursestrings,

My mom finally agreed to let me work a part-time job after school, as long as my grades don't drop. I can't decide if I should work for a lady down the street helping her care for Erin, her 3-year old, or start a jewelry business going door to door. I figure if I sell three bracelets a week, I can make twice as much as I would working for my neighbor.

Sincerely,
Jewel Orsit

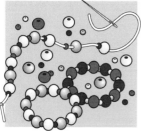

Dear Jewel,

It's great that you have a couple of job opportunities! You do need to weigh the pros and cons of working for someone else and having a boss versus working alone. You have already determined one of the advantages to working on your own, which is the possibility of making more money. But there are other considerations. With an employer, you don't have to worry about purchasing supplies or finding customers. It also allows you to have a set schedule, such as babysitting twice a week, with steady income. On the other hand, if you love making jewelry and meeting new people, that business might work just as well for you.

Miss Pursestrings

Dear Miss Pursestrings,

My friend and I have been in business for a year, selling fresh lemonade on weekends. We do pretty well, but I'd like to find a way to make more money. Any suggestions?

Sincerely,
Leigh Monade

Dear Leigh,

You might want to ask your customers what other products they would like. If you are open year-round, try offering hot beverages such as coffee or hot cocoa in the fall, and fruit juices or soda in the summer. This strategy can work for other businesses as well. If you mow lawns in the summer, try offering a raking service in the fall and snow shoveling in the winter.

Miss Pursestrings

❋A NICE PRICE❋

Now that you're considering your own business for extra cash, you're probably wondering how much you can expect to earn. And your customers will want to know how much you charge before hiring you to do work. How can you decide what your job is worth?

1. Check around to see what other people are being paid for similar work. For example, if babysitters in your area are making $3 an hour, you should make your rates similar to stay competitive. But remember not to price yourself too low! "A worker is worthy of his wages" (Luke 10:7).

2. Decide how you want to be paid. You could charge by the hour or by the job. If you charge by the hour, you must work steadily and do a great job so your customer doesn't think you're trying to charge too much. But if you can work well at a quick pace, you might make more money by charging by the job.

Nifty Thrifty Tip

Before ordering on-line or from catalogs, check the shipping charges. You might find that they are not such great deals after all!

3. Make sure your rates are low enough so people will hire you, but high enough that it will be worth your while to do the job.

4. How hard is the work? The more difficult, the more money!

5. Once you set a price, stick to it. If you charge by the "task," don't change the price, even if it takes you longer to do. (Just keep this in mind the next time you offer to do it.)

6. If you have little or no experience, set your price a little lower. As you gain experience, you can raise your price.

7. Make sure your price covers the cost of supplies and your time. Use the What to Charge form on page 189 if you need more help figuring out what to charge for a job.

Green Back FACT

In the early 1800s, the Secretary of the Treasury got letters asking him to put "God" on U.S. coins. Many mottoes were suggested, such as "Our Country, Our God," "God, Our Trust" and "Our God and Our Country." The leaders finally decided on "In God We Trust" and it first appeared on the two-cent coin in 1864.

☀WHICH ONE ARE YOU?☀

Making money isn't all about knowing what to do and what to charge – it's also about you, the worker. What kind of energy do you have for this job? Are you footloose and fancy free and want to just make some quick cash so you can use the rest of your time for other hobbies and interests? Or are you an entrepreneur, someone who's a go-getter and wants to work hard? To find out, check off all of the characteristics that apply to you and see which one you are!

Employee

Fun-loving
Natural follower
Likes to work in groups
Likes to know what to expect
Enjoys a fixed paycheck
Likes having a boss
Practical
Follows directions

Entrepreneur

Adventurous
Natural Leader
Likes to work alone
Likes flexibility
Wants pay based on success
Likes being the boss
Risk-taker
Experimental

HELP WANTED:
❋PARTNERING WITH A FRIEND❋

If you don't like working alone, teaming up with a partner may be the answer for you! It's twice the fun and your job will get done in half the time. Plus, people like hiring a team because they know the work will be finished faster.

But remember: your friendship is worth more than money, so keep things fair. Equal work means equal pay. If both of you share the work, split the earnings equally (after you cover expenses). And be sure to trade off jobs from time to time so one of you doesn't get stuck doing the tough stuff.

TAKIN' CARE OF BUSINESS
Purple Thread
(Based on Acts 16:14)

Sara never saw herself as poor, though by America's standard she was. Her mom's paycheck from working the nightshift barely covered the groceries for Sara and her two brothers and three sisters.

The area where Sara and her family lived was rough at best. Most kids brought up there tended to stay poor when they got older, or they got into robbery, or dealing drugs. Sara's own father was in prison for selling drugs.

Even though Sara wanted to get a job so she could help her mom, she couldn't because she already had one – taking care of her little brothers and sisters. Sara's mom was so tired from working that Sara was in charge of the cooking, cleaning and laundry at her house.

One day Sara saw some beautiful bluish-purple embroidery thread in her mom's sewing basket. While she watched TV, Sara twisted and knotted the thread to make tassels for her siblings' pencils. Their friends at school commented how much they liked them and asked how much they cost. Suddenly, Sara found herself earning several dollars a week from making tassels for schoolmates.

One day, Sara noticed she had quite a bit of money in the jar on her dresser. Then she remembered a commercial she saw on TV asking for people to help feed hungry children.

Sara asked her mom if she could sponsor a child. Her mom joyfully answered, "Honey, someday you're going to have the world eating out of your hands!"

Sara smiled with pride that God would use her to help someone less fortunate.

On one of Paul's journeys, he met a woman named Lydia. She sold purple thread for making the tassels on prayer shawls. This thread was very valuable! After learning about Jesus, she was baptized and invited Paul to her home. She knew Paul's message of salvation was important, and she wanted to support his ministry. So Lydia donated purple thread for Paul to use in his tent-making business, and to sell. You can read about it in Acts 16:14.

The next time you see something as simple as thread, remember that God can use even the smallest act to do great things for Him!

To Think About!

How can your business help others?

Prayer

Dear God, I don't have a lot of time to work because of school and all my activities. But will You help me anyway? I know if I am productive and get organized, I'll get good results, with Your help. In Jesus' name, amen.

$ CHAPTER EIGHT $

Hot Dogs
99¢ ea.

OPEN FOR BUSINESS!

Are you ready to start your own business? Have you chosen a moneymaker that matches your personality and talents? If so, use the Business Plan form on page 190 to jot down all the details of your business. But before you fill out the form, read on for some insider tips on running a really good business.

☀THE NAME GAME☀

You need to choose a name for your business. Have fun as you decide on a creative name, but make sure it is something people can easily match to the type of business you have. For example, "The Brittany Company" might look great, but it doesn't tell anyone what you are selling. On the other hand, "Brittany's Brownies" lets the

customer know what you are selling, and it sounds good, too!

When you are trying to come up with a business name, think through these questions:

What do you do?

Who are you?

What is the location of your business?

What type of service are you offering?

What is unique about your service or product?

☀ LOCATION, LOCATION, LOCATION ☀

These three words are key for businesses that sell products instead of services. For example, your yard sale isn't going to do too well if it is on a quiet street with no signs. But if you put up signs on busy streets with arrows pointing your direction, people will find you.

If your business is mobile, such as a food stand, take it to your customers! Set up shop on the corner of a busy street or at a park, school, beach or outside your mom or dad's business. The more people who see you and what you have to offer, the more product you are likely to sell.

☀ A GOOD START ☀

Before you spend a lot of money on supplies for your business, make a list of everything you really need. Try to use what you already have at home first. For example, if you are starting a babysitting business, gather old – but fun! – toys that are unused around your house. (But don't steal your little sister's games!) Or if you are starting a gardening business, ask your parents if you can borrow a rake and bucket before you go to buy new ones. Using what you  have is important, because the less you spend on supplies, the more money you can save so you make a profit!

If you will be selling a product, you should "test market" it before you open your business and spend money on supplies. For example, if you're selling cookies, you should have family and friends test them first. It might take you a few batches to get your recipe the way you want it, but once your testers approve, you will know you have a huge hit!

Nifty Thrifty Tip

Use unusual ways to get your customers' attention. Tie balloons on a garage sale sign, give out buttons with your company's name on them, wear a costume to advertise a special event or give out samples of your latest creation.

Once you have a solid supply list, you will need money to buy your supplies so you can get started. Just buy a few supplies at first until you see how your business goes. You can always buy more later!

Perhaps you have enough savings to pay for your start-up costs. If not, ask your parents if they will loan you the money. Promise to pay them back after you have made the money – and do it! Remember, if you are faithful over a little, God will bless you with much more.

❊MAKE THE RIGHT CALL❊

There might be times when you'll need to call a customer for more information about a job or to reschedule an appointment. If the thought of talking to an adult on the phone makes you feel like soap bubbles are popping in your stomach, or your voice shakes like you're sitting on a washing machine on the spin cycle – calm down! There's nothing to fear. Most adults will be understanding and patient if you explain why you're calling.

Here are some tips for using the phone:

1. Speak slowly and clearly. You want to be heard, so be sure to speak in complete sentences – don't mumble!

2. If the adult sounds busy and seems to be rushing to get off the phone, ask for a good time to call back. If you get a time to call back, repeat the time and date and say you will be returning the call.

3. If the person you are trying to reach isn't home, leave a message with whomever answers the phone, or on the answering machine. Be sure to leave your name, the time you called, your telephone number and the reason for your call. If your call is not returned in a timely manner, call back.

4. Be sure to have pen and paper ready to take notes from your conversation.

5. If someone suggests calling another person who may be interested in your business, do call. If you get business from that person, thank your original contact for the referral.

☀LET YOUR FINGERS DO THE WALKING☀

Did you know that calling directory assistance for a phone number is expensive? Instead, use the phone directories provided by your local telephone company. The white pages list residential and business names and phone numbers. The

Yellow Pages list businesses in alphabetical order according to the types of services or products they offer. For instance, if you were looking for a craft supply store, you would look under "C" for "Craft." Then under "Craft" you would see several categories, such as Galleries, Dealers, Supplies-retail and Wholesale, etc. Under Supplies-retail, several stores could be listed with the stores' locations and phone numbers. Now you can find the store nearest you! Many businesses place ads within their listings with more information. You can also use the index in the back of the book for finding what you need.

Here are some more tips for using phone books:

1. Names are listed A-Z by last name, then by first name. For example, if you are looking for Candice Jones, first find the beginning of the "J" listings. Then, look for "J-o" until you find "Jones." Now look at the first names within the Jones listings. Look until you come to the "C." Carefully look until you reach "Candice." If there are several Candice Joneses in the book, check the address to verify the one you are trying to reach.

Nifty Thrifty Tip

Have repeat customers by taking care of your customers. Send your customers thank-you notes for their business.

2. Check the blue pages for government listings such as post offices, libraries and government offices.

3. Most phone books also have lists of zip codes for your state, in case you need to mail letters.

4. Check the front of the phone book for frequently used numbers – police, fire and other important numbers.

☀GET THE WORD OUT☀

Word of mouth is the best way to let people know you're in business and ready to work. Tell everyone you see: family, church friends, neighbors, teachers and your parents' co-workers. Once you have a following of devoted customers, they will tell others, who will tell others, who will still tell others, until you are swarming in business!

Good Cents
Scripture

But remember the Lord your God, for it is he who gives you the ability to produce wealth.

~ Deuteronomy 8:18

Dear Miss Pursestrings,

My friend and I wanted to make some fast cash before Christmas so we started a snow-shoveling business. We have been all over our neighborhood and we just can't seem to get anyone to say yes. How can we convince people we will do a good job?

Sincerely,
Freeza Little

Dear Freeza,

Teamwork is the best way to get the job done quickly and safely, but first you need to defrost your business. Customers who say no may not necessarily mean no. It might be they don't have the money right now to hire you. Ask if you can come back another time to do it for them. Also, help them warm up to you by telling them about other happy customers (in your case, it may be your own parents!). You can also leave them a business card with your phone number so they can call you later. And don't forget to ask for "leads" – names of others who might need your service. That way you can approach the lead with "Mrs. Jones suggested I contact you." Before you know it, your business will start to snowball!

Miss Pursestrings

Dear Miss Pursestrings,

It's no use! I give up! I wanted to buy a CD player with the earnings from my dog-walking service, but I just haven't been able to get any jobs. I hung flyers all around the neighborhood. I even went door-to-door trying to drum up business. I guess I'm just not a good salesperson. What should I do now?

Sincerely,
Aleasha Day

Dear Aleasha,

When it comes to selling, no one does it as well as kids! In fact, you've been doing it all your life, but just didn't know it – such as when you convinced your mom to let you keep the stray kitten you found on the way home from school, or persuaded her to order a pizza instead of having leftover meatloaf for dinner. Although you may never have given it much thought, you were actually selling your idea to her! And those same techniques (with the exception of begging, pleading and drooling!) that you used on your mom and dad can be used on customers. You need to convince them to use your service!

Miss Pursestrings

☀ TOOLS OF THE TRADE ☀

Depending on the type of business you have, these tools could be helpful in staying organized and getting the word out.

Price Tags

If you are having a garage sale or you will be displaying your items for sale in a shop, you should mark them with price tags. Customers want to know how much things cost without having to ask. Plain, inexpensive stickers make good price tags.

Customer Receipts

Let your customer know you are serious about your business by using receipts. You can either make your own on a computer or you can buy them already printed at an office supply store. If you buy them, get the ones with carbon paper so you make a copy for your customer and yourself at the same time. A good record keeper makes a good business person! A sample customer receipt is on page 191.

Order Forms

Will you be taking orders for your business? If so, keep some order forms by the phone for when customers call.

Service Agreements

Having an agreement with your customers will help you avoid misunderstandings. Be sure your agreement includes:

1. Your name, address and phone number.

2. Customer's name, address, and phone number.

3. A clear description of the job and what you will do.

4. The date when the job will be finished.

5. The amount the customer has agreed to pay.

6. How the customer has agreed to pay and when (cash, check, barter, etc.).

7. Places for both you and the customer to sign.

Business Cards

Tell others about your business with colorful business cards. Don't forget to include personal information (name, address, phone), so customers can contact you. If you have a computer and a color printer, you can easily print your cards and cut them out. Or for a personal touch, make your cards by hand and color them yourself! A business card pattern is on page 186.

Door Hangers

Tell everyone in the neighborhood about
your business with door hangers. You can make

your own on a computer, then go door-to-door and hang them.
That way you get your ad to those who aren't home or you
don't know. A door hanger pattern is on page 192.

Ad Flyers

To really get noticed, design some eye-catching flyers or
posters that describe your business. Hang them on bulletin
boards at church, the YMCA, grocery stores, colleges, health
clubs, libraries – or wherever your customers might be. Check
out ads in newspapers and magazines for clever ways to write
your ads.

DO'S AND DON'TS FOR SUCCESSFUL BUSINESS OWNERS

DO a little extra. Make customers feel like
they're getting their money's worth.

DON'T keep them waiting. Provide good
service in a timely manner.

DO your best. Make customers glad they
hired you.

DON'T argue with customers. Handle
complaints by trying to do what
customers expect.

DO all that you can do. God rewards those
who are diligent!

DON'T ever leave a job unfinished. Get the
job done!

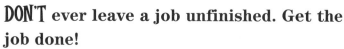

☀DRESS FOR SUCCESS☀

Now that you are a professional in business for herself, it's important to dress the part. A simple rule of thumb to remember is this: wear comfortable clothing that looks neat and clean. That doesn't mean wearing your Sunday best, but always think about wearing apparel that fits the job description.

For example, if you are doing a car wash, wear clothes that you don't mind getting wet. If you are painting or doing yard work, you definitely should wear clothing your mom won't mind your getting soiled. You also should protect your skin from sun and nature when working outdoors. If you are trimming shrubs and will be working around bushes with thorns, wear a long-sleeved shirt.

☀SALES 101☀

There are several ways to get people to buy. Try these simple steps when approaching a customer about your product or service:

1. Ask God to help you to be honest in your work.

2. Smile and speak in a kind, friendly voice.

3. Tell customers how your product or service will help them. Offer several suggestions for using your product or service.

4. Try to convince the customer to buy now by adding something special and saying "for a limited time only"!

5. Don't be shy about asking people to buy. Expect them to say yes!

WORK IT OUT

Use the words below to fill in the blanks. Find out what God says about a diligent worker.

plans   diligent

profit   haste   poverty

"The _____ of the _____ lead to

_____, as surely as _____ leads to

_____." ~ Proverbs 21:5

TAKIN' CARE OF BUSINESS
Something Borrowed
(Based on 2 Kings 6:5-7)

The Jacobs twin sisters' lawn care and shrub-trimming business was thriving. Both Jessica and Jaime were excited about their business, especially because they both loved the outdoors.

The twins had saved up enough to buy their own mower, but they still needed more equipment to trim hedges. They begged their father to allow them to use his cordless trimmers. Reluctantly, he agreed. He made them promise to return them to the garage after each use.

"These trimmers are very expensive," he explained. The twins agreed that they would take care of them.

The next day, the girls worked on Mrs. Jones' yard. Jessica trimmed with the trimmers, while Jaime carried cuttings to the trash can. But while she was trimming, Jessica swatted at a mosquito attacking her arm – which made her accidentally drop the trimmers into a pond next to her.

"Oh, no! Daddy's trimmers!" Jessica cried.

Just then, Mr. Jones walked up and saw the girls.

"What's wrong?" he asked.

The girls explained what had happened.

Mr. Jones got a long fishing pole from his barn and used it to retrieve the trimmers from the water.

"Oh, thank you so much, Mr. Jones," the girls gratefully sang out. "We borrowed those from our dad."

"Well, in that case we had better clean this up and get it running again," Mr. Jones said with a smile. Relieved, the girls thanked him again for his help.

The Bible tells the story of a man who borrowed an expensive tool – called an "iron axe" – to cut down poles for Elisha, the prophet. While he was cutting down trees, the iron axe accidentally fell into the Jordan River! The man knew that if he didn't return the tool, he would gain a huge debt he couldn't repay. He would be sold into slavery until his debt was paid!

But God stepped in. When Elisha threw a stick in the water, the axe immediately floated to the surface! Read all about it in 2 Kings 6:5-7.

God understands when bad things happen. He is there to help us through it.

To Think About!

How has God helped you out of tough spots in your business or in other parts of your life?

Prayer

Dear God, help me always to do the best job I can, because I know You are watching. Help me to be a good worker. Bless the work of my hands. In Jesus' name, amen.

Green Back FACT

The same day the Declaration of Independence was signed, the Continental Congress charged Benjamin Franklin, Thomas Jefferson and John Adams with creating a seal for the United States. The final artwork took six years, three committees and many revisions before its final approval on June 20, 1782. This seal is still on our dollar bill today.

$ CHAPTER NINE $

FUN WAYS TO EARN CASH

Are you willing to work but not sure what to do? Here are some great ideas for jumpstarting your business. Just be sure to check with your parents before you plan – and especially before you give out your family's phone number, home address or email address. The symbol before each job tells you how it matches your interests from the quiz on pages 105-107.

BALLOON STORY TIME CLUB

Make books come alive at your Balloon Story Time Club for kids!

What You Need

children's picture books

a chair

What to Do

1. Plan your club. For example, will it be a one-day event or a certain day each week? Where will it be held?

2. Decide how many books you will read, and which ones. If you have a younger sibling, find out his or her favorite books – other little kids probably will like them, too.

3. How long will your club last? Most kids can sit through two picture books before getting fidgety. Consider doing a short activity between books, such as doing fun exercises, singing songs or playing games.

4. Decide how much to charge for each child.

5. Make flyers advertising your club and hang them at libraries, schools, day care centers and around your neighborhood. Be sure to include your name and telephone number, the date and time for the club, the books you will be reading, and how much it costs. Ask people to contact you for reservations so you know how many kids to expect.
6. Decorate the story area with balloons to match your theme.
7. The best book readers make the characters come alive as they read. Use a different voice for each character. After each book, ask the kids questions about the story: "What was your favorite part?" "Who was your favorite character?"

Tip Jar!

☼ If you run out of books to read, ask the kids to bring their favorite books to a club meeting. Let each child tell why the book is his or her favorite.

☼ Have the kids come dressed as their favorite story book characters. Let each child tell everyone about his or her character and act out a part from the story. You should get dressed up, too!

☼ Make the Balloon Story Time Club a true club: create a membership card for each kid and put a sticker on it every time he or she comes to the club.

BALLPARK BITES

The best hot dogs are those at the ballpark – when everyone is hungry!

What You Need

hot dogs

hot dog buns

condiments (ketchup, mustard, relish)

soda

water

cooler

ice

napkins

poster board

marker

table

chair

What to Do

1. Use a marker and poster board to make a sign for your hot dogs and drinks. List out what you have and how much each item costs.

2. With a parent's assistance, fill a sauce pan with water and bring it to a boil. Drop in the hot dogs, cover the pan and remove it from heat. Allow it to stand for 7 to 9 minutes.

3. Or, heat the hot dogs in the microwave. Place one hotdog in a small dish with ½ cup of water. Cover and heat for 1.5 minutes.

4. Wrap hotdogs in foil to keep them warm.

5. Set up shop at a baseball game or park (get permission first).

❋ **Buy snack-size bags of chips in bulk and offer them with a dog and soda at a special combo price.**

❋ **Buy store brand sodas – they're cheaper.**

❋ **Add to your menu with popcorn. It is an easy snack to make and sell in small paper lunch bags.**

❋ **Candy or homebaked goods are also great sellers at ballgames and parks!**

COIN COASTERS

These simple coasters with coin imprints make great gifts. They are sure to impress your family and friends!

What You Need

coins

self-hardening clay

cardboard

acrylic paint

varnish

wax paper

rolling pin   *continued on next page…*

What You Need (continued)

butter knife

ribbon (optional)

What to Do

1. Cut out a 4-inch cardboard square to use as a template.

2. Spread a sheet of wax paper on your work surface.

3. Roll a 2½-inch ball of clay to ¼-inch thickness.

4. Arrange some coins on the clay and press them into it with the rolling pin making a distinctive impression.

5. Lay the cardboard template over the clay and cut around the cardboard using a butter knife.

6. Lift the coaster and set it aside to dry for a day. Rework the leftover clay and make more coasters.

7. After the coasters dry, paint an acrylic varnish over them and allow to dry.

8. After the varnish dries, dab white paint on the coins' impressions to highlight them. Then add another coat of varnish and allow to dry.

Tip Jar!

✳ Tie together four Coin Coasters with a red ribbon and sell them as sets.

✳ Use leaves, twigs or pine needles instead of coins as variations.

✳ Go door-to-door with sets of Coin Coasters just before Christmas. Tell customers that your Coin Coasters make great gifts for hard-to-shop-for people!

CREATIVE CARDS

Put your computer to work and create greeting cards for birthdays and holidays!

What You Need

8½" x 11" card stock

computer

color printer

envelopes

computer software (optional)

What to Do

1. Make a selection of greeting cards using your computer. You can make them using your own creativity, or let greeting card software do the work for you. Include a variety of holidays, birthdays and themes. Use stickers, ribbon and lace to make the cards extra special.

2. Decide how much to charge for your cards. Price your cards below store-bought cards to entice buyers.

3. Sell cards from your pre-made selection, but also offer personalized cards. When you take orders for personalized cards, find out how they should read, if they should be printed in special colors and how many the customers need.

4. Keep copies of personalized card designs in case your customers want to reorder.

※ **Sell cards in sets of 8, including envelopes. Tie the bundle with a pretty ribbon.**

※ **Use scrapbooking scissors with special edges to give the cards a custom touch.**

※ **Use photographs, pressed flowers or pieces of fabric on the cards.**

※ **Make confetti and add it as an extra feature to sell with your cards.**

THE CUPID CORPORATION

Play matchmaker with your family, neighbors and friends! Your customers will write the notes, but you do the delivery.

What You Need

valentines

valentine candy

pink paper

blank envelopes

note pad

What to Do

1. Decide what you will charge. Make or buy valentines and write your business information inside them.

2. Spread the word around the neighborhood and at school about your new business a few weeks before Valentine's Day.

3. A week or so before Valentine's Day, begin to take orders.

4. Have a form for customers to fill out. They should write their name, the recipient's name and any special message they want on the valentine.

5. Ask if the customer would like to add candy or a special item to the message (for an extra charge).

6. Dress in red (or even a cupid costume!) for delivering everyone's valentines.

※ **Tell everyone you know at school. This is sure to be a big hit with your friends!**

※ **Collect the money at the time the order is placed.**

※ **Buy pink paper and envelopes for customers who want to send longer messages.**

※ **Use your bike for faster delivery service.**

CURB COMMUNICATOR

Paint house numbers on street curbs so houseguests and emergency vehicles can find the houses they need.

What You Need

three sets of 3-inch stencils

paint brush

spray paint

tape

continued on next page...

What You Need (continued)

poster board

box

What to Do

1. Decide how much you will charge for each set of curb numbers.

2. Cut a rectangular shape (hole) from the poster board as a template you will hold to keep paint off of grass and roads.

3. Clean the curb surface before starting.

4. Paint inside your rectangular template with white paint.

5. Tape the number stencils on the template to hold them in place, then spray black paint.

6. Carefully remove the stencils.

❊ **Explain to the customers that these numbers will help police cars and fire and ambulance trucks find everyone's houses easier and faster.**

❊ **The numbers will also help delivery services find their homes easier, as well as friends and family.**

❊ **If you are creative, offer to add small designs to the curb numbers for an extra fee. Just be sure the numbers still can be read easily.**

DOG WALKER

Dogs need fresh air and exercise, too! This service will appeal to busy people who might not have enough time to walk their dogs every day.

What You Need

dog leash

walking shoes

plastic sack

pet treats

What to Do

1. Decide on a fee for service. Have different prices for daily and multi-day walking.

2. Contact your neighbors and let them know that you are available for dog walking. Also hang flyers in local pet stores.

3. Arrive early at the client's house so you can get to know the dog.

4. Scoop up poop with a plastic sack and throw it in the trash – you don't want to leave it behind for someone else to step in!

Tip Jar!

❋ **Always use a leash.**

❋ **Don't walk more than two dogs at a time or you will go doggone crazy with criss-crossed leashes!**

❋ **Give the dogs treats for good behavior (but check with the owners first).**

DRESSING DESIGNER

Here's a great idea that will add zip to a busy family's dinner salad!

What You Need

1 cup olive oil

1 cup white wine vinegar

2 tablespoons dried herbs or ½ cup of fresh herbs

salt

pepper

salad bottles

paper

ribbon

What to Do

1. Remove the labels from used salad dressing bottles and wash them in a dishwasher or in very hot water.

2. Choose the combination of herbs you want to use for your salad dressing. Here are some ideas: dill/chive/peppercorn, basil/garlic, basil/chive, mint/rosemary, garlic/chive, thyme/sage or rosemary/thyme. If you use fresh herbs, wash them and pat them dry.

3. Combine all of the ingredients and pour them into the bottles.

4. Tie a colorful tag tied around the bottle with directions for use: "Shake well before using. Refrigerate after each use."

5. Make a few "sample" bottles to take door to door in your neighborhood or apartment complex.

6. Take orders and let the customers know when you will be delivering the dressing.

7. Collect the money when the product has been delivered.

✶ **Store your dressing in the refrigerator when it is not on display.**

✶ **Make a menu of herb combinations and take special orders for them.**

✶ **These dressings also make great meat marinades.**

✶ **Try using red wine vinegar for a splash of color.**

FANCY FACE PAINTER

Use your creativity to make a child smile. Some adults might want a little decorating, too!

What You Need

face painting crayons or paint

mirror

poster board

two folding chairs

What to Do

1. Decide what you will charge for each face. You could have different fees depending on the detail of the artwork.

2. Make flyers to advertise your service. Offer to work at fairs, carnivals, craft fairs, birthday parties or other special events. Hang your flyers at party stores and schools.

3. Use poster board to make a bright, colorful poster that will draw attention to your booth (but you don't *really* need a booth – just chairs for you and your customer!).

4. On your sign or another piece of poster board, draw sample designs so kids can choose what they want. Also offer to do custom designs.

5. Paint your own face as a way to show people your work.

6. Use your mirror to show kids how they look when you're finished.

 ❊ **Wear colorful clothing so you match the party mood, or even dress in a clown outfit to give kids extra entertainment.**

❊ **Go to football and baseball games. Fans will want their team's colors and mascots painted on their faces.**

❊ **Ask kids as they are walking by if they want to have their faces painted. They'll almost always say yes! While you're working on one child, others will gather around to watch – and then they'll want theirs done, too.**

FLYER DISTRIBUTOR

Be the wings for local advertisers by helping them spread the word about their businesses!

What You Need

- paper
- markers
- phone
- computer
- backpack
- bike

What to Do

1. Decide how much to charge for your service. Most companies will want to pay you by the number of houses you visit.

2. Hang flyers to advertise your service.

3. Call local businesses and let them know you are available to distribute flyers for their businesses. (They may even ask you to design them!)

✷ **Advertise at the local copy center.**

✷ **Hang flyers on door knobs, attach them to newspapers or put them on car windshields.**

✷ **If you are going door-to-door, add a charge for any sales pitch the business wants you to give.**

GARDEN MARKET

If you have a green thumb, you can watch your money grow!

What You Need

seed packets for flowers, herbs or vegetables

potting soil

plastic cups

sunny windowsill

shallow trays

What to Do

1. Fill small starter pots or one long shallow tray with potting soil and plant the seeds. (You can buy pots, trays and potting soil at a local home improvement store.)

2. Lightly water the pots and place them in a sunny window. Check them daily to make sure the soil does not get too dry. But don't over water them either by causing the soil to turn to mud!

3. For best results, follow the directions for your geographical area on the backs of the seed packets.

4. Decide what to charge for each plant (check with local garden shops to see how much they charge for starter plants).

5. Make a sign with the types of plants you have and what they cost.

6. When your plants are several inches high, sell them in front of your house in the evenings when adults are coming home from work, and on weekends.

 ※ **Suggest to customers multiple uses for herbs and flowers, such as herbs for cooking, drying and hanging, adding to hot baths, making homemade soaps, pressing and decorating.**

※ **Wrap some of the plants in colored cellophane and tie with ribbon in case customers want to use them for gifts.**

※ **Start your own cuttings from mature plants (for additional information read** THE CHRISTIAN KIDS' GARDENING GUIDE**).**

GIFT WRAP GIRL

Set up a stand by a store around Christmas and wrap gifts for a fee.

What You Need

gift wrap, assorted

gift bags, assorted

ribbons, bows, etc.

colored tissue paper

boxes, variety of sizes

scissors

tape

What to Do

1. Decide what to charge for your service. Go to some stores that offer gift-wrapping and see what they charge. Also, take note of the styles they offer.

2. Make an easy-to-read sign that shows your services and fees.

3. Wrap several empty boxes so you can display your gift wrap, bow and ribbon options.

4. Talk to store managers about your service. You will need permission to set up in front of their stores.

5. Be sure to dress neatly and keep a clean work area.

❋ **For an extra fee, tie small toys or decorative items to the tops of the packages.**

❋ **Have other items available for sale (such as some of the gifts in this chapter).**

❋ **Plan ahead: buy discounted gift wrap at after-Christmas sales to use the next year.**

❋ **Offer your services during other holidays such as Mother's Day and Father's Day.**

HOUSE SITTING

This is a great summer job for when people go on vacation. You can make money just by watching their houses!

What You Need

memo pad

What to Do

1. Taking care of pets, watering plants, and bringing in the mail and newspapers are all things you can do for customers while they are away.

2. Decide on a fee. You could charge by the day, by the week or by the trip.

3. Before your customers leave, make sure you have their house keys, alarm system codes and phone numbers where they can be reached. Ask them to write down any special instructions for pets. Be sure to ask for their vet's name and phone number, in case of an emergency.

4. Ask your customers to tell their neighbors that you will be watching their houses so the neighbors don't think you are a burglar!

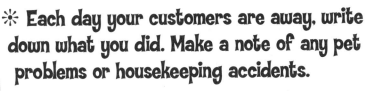

※ **Each day your customers are away, write down what you did. Make a note of any pet problems or housekeeping accidents.**

※ **Keep your customers' house keys in a safe place.**

※ **Before you leave your customers' houses, always double check to make sure all doors and windows are locked.**

Nifty Thrifty Tip

Need a Web site for your business or favorite hobby? Check services that allow you to build your own Web site for free!

JAMMING DJ

Everyone loves a good DJ – and you will love this super-fun way to make money!

What You Need

variety of CDs

powerful boom box or sound system

microphone

What to Do

1. Decide on a pricing plan for your service. Will you charge by the hour or by the event?

2. Make flyers and pass them around at schools and in your neighborhood. Be sure to leave some flyers at music and party stores.

3. When customers call, ask what kind of music they want you to play. Also, ask how long the party is and how you should dress.

4. Arrive about an hour before the party to set up your equipment. After the party, help the hosts tidy up.

Tip Jar!

✳ **Holidays are a good time to advertise this service because more people have parties around those times.**

✳ **Talk to people who rent out rooms to let them know about your business. Ask them if they could recommend you to customers.**

✳ At an event where you are DJ-ing, leave flyers on the tables so others can find out about you and call you for parties.

✳ Have fun and talk to the guests. Encourage them to join in the activities at the party.

✳ If you have a karaoke machine (or you can borrow or rent one), offer to add karaoke to the party for an additional fee.

✳ If you are a good singer, add singing to your list of services.

LEAF IT TO ME RAKING SERVICE

During fall, keep the money coming in with a leaf-raking business.

What You Need

rake

garbage bags

What to Do

1. Decide what you will charge per yard.

2. Make flyers or business cards advertising your service.

3. Walk around the neighborhood looking for houses with lots of leaves in their yards. Knock and ask them if you can rake their leaves, or leave a flyer.

4. Schedule a return visit before the end of the season.

✳ **Offer to make weekly visits for quick yard touch-ups.**

✳ **The early bird gets the worm: before winter hits, let your customers know you are available to shovel the sidewalks and driveways.**

LIP SMACKIN' GOOD! COOKBOOK

If you like cooking up tasty treats, make your own cookbook.

What You Need

recipes

paper

computer

printer

What to Do

1. Ask friends and family to contribute recipes to your cookbook.

2. Organize the recipes into categories, such as meats, vegetables and desserts.

3. Type everything on the computer.

4. Add clip-art and pictures if you have them.

5. Take the pages to a copy shop. Have the books printed and bound (most cookbooks have a plastic binding).

6. Sell your cookbooks to family, neighbors and friends.

Tip Jar!

- Use colored paper for the cover to make it bright and attractive.
- Have the pages laminated for durability if your budget allows.
- To help promote your cookbook, hold a bake sale with desserts from the recipes. Tell customers that they can find the recipes for all the desserts in your cookbook.

LOVELY LAWNS

This is a business that will keep you busy all summer long!

What You Need

paper

markers

lawn mower

lawn trimmer

garden tools

broom

rake

garbage bags

What to Do

1. Decide what you will charge and what that fee will include. Will you mow and trim? Will you weed the flower beds? Will you water?

2. Make flyers to leave on your neighbors' doors advertising your business.

3. Leave your customers' yards looking as beautiful as possible – they will be your best ads for more business!

※ **Use a calendar to keep track of your jobs.**

※ **Recruit friends to help you and share the profits.**

※ **Wear a headset so you can listen to music while you work to make the time go by faster.**

 **MISS CLEAN**

If you are good at organizing, you will really "clean up" at this job. And you can listen to tunes while you do it!

What You Need

   work gloves

   broom

   dust pan

   trash bags

What to Do

1. Decide what you will charge. If you're not sure how long a job will take, figure on an hourly rate. But if you can estimate the time, charge a flat fee.

2. Advertise by hanging flyers in your neighborhood.

3. Begin the job by removing big items that are blocking the space.

4. Remove trash, but be sure to ask the customer when you aren't sure whether an item is trash or not.

5. Sweep the floor.

6. Organize items in groups, such as yard tools, outdoor equipment, pool items, paint, tools, etc.

❋ **Wear gloves to protect your hands. If the room is extremely dusty, wear a dust mask.**

❋ **Bring a headset so you can listen to music while you work.**

❋ **Ask the customer for referrals of friends who could also use your service.**

MOTHER'S HELPER

Not sure if you're ready to babysit by yourself? This is a great way to get used to babysitting because the moms will still be around if you need them.

What You Need

paper

markers

bag of toys

What to Do

1. Decide on your fees. It is probably best to charge by the hour as you would with babysitting.

2. Hang colorful flyers at libraries and grocery stores where busy moms will see them.

3. Bring toys, games and activities for the kids to play with you.

4. When you arrive to work, check with the mother for special instructions on snacks, naps, where the can kids play, etc.

※ **The moms are paying you to give them time to get things done, so try not to interrupt them.**

※ **In addition to active toys, bring books to read to the kids for quiet times.**

※ **Don't forget to cross-sell your services: ask the mom if she'd like to hire you for cleaning or yardwork!**

MOVERS-ON-THE-GO

This business will keep you, well, moving! Help neighbors pack and unpack when they move out or in.

What You Need

work gloves

paper

markers

What to Do

1. Decide what you will charge. An hourly rate is practical, but you could charge by the job if you know how many hours it will take.

156

2. Hang flyers around the neighborhood to let people know about your service. Be sure to put your rates on the flyers.

3. Watch for moving vans in your neighborhood. Go over and introduce yourself to the people who are moving and tell them that you're available to help for a fee.

4. Work quickly, but be careful when you handle breakable items. Let adults carry heavier things.

✳ **Be friendly and polite.**

✳ **If your customers are moving in, let them know that you're also available to unpack boxes and organize items.**

✳ **Offer to do other jobs while you're there, such as cleaning, yardwork or babysitting.**

⦙ MUSIC TEACHER ⦙

If music is your thing, or you know how to play an instrument, you can make money teaching others.

What You Need

paper

markers

sheet music

instrument

What to Do

1. Decide what you will charge. Hourly rates are most common for music lessons.

2. Make flyers and hang them at music stores, the band or music department at school and on bulletin boards at your local library.

3. Depending on the instrument, you may want to meet at the student's house or at your house.

4. Be patient and give your students the extra attention they need to learn how to play.

❋ **Offer one free lesson to try to get new customers.**

❋ **Sign up customers by the month so you will know they are committed.**

❋ **Hold a recital at the end of a few months of lessons so your students' parents can see how their money has paid off!**

MY MUSIC STORE

Collect your favorite music and make money at the same time!

What You Need

used records, cassettes and CDs

poster board

markers

What to Do

1. Search everywhere for cheap, used records, cassettes and CDs. Garage sales are a great source! Make a deal by offering one price for all the records they have.

2. Set prices based on the value of your items. Research the Internet for prices and to find out if any of the items are collectibles. They may be worth more than you think!

3. Hang up flyers about your sale a few days before you have it so people will know about it.

4. Use poster board to make bright, colorful signs that will lead your customers to the music sale.

❊ **Set up a booth at a flea market and display your items.**

❊ **As an alternative to having a sale, you could take your items to a music resale shop and sell them to the stores.**

NATURAL COSMETICS COMPANY

Your friends will love these! Here are several different products to offer your customers for themselves or as gifts. Tell them, "Let the sweet fragrance of roses go with you all day!"

Ways to Market Your Cosmetics

1. Invite girlfriends over and have a makeover party!

2. Go door to door in your neighborhood. (The #1 cosmetics company in the world does it that way!)

3. Give away samples at school and club meetings.

ROSE BODY POWDER

What You Need

(All of these ingredients can be found at your local natural food store, craft store or online.)

1 cup dried rose petals

1 cup dried lavender petals

1 lb. arrowroot powder

rose oil

large mixing bowl

containers with lids

What to Do

1. In a large mixing bowl, crush the rose and lavender petals between your fingers until they are powdery. Or, you can use a mortar to blend them together.

Nifty Thrifty Tip

Check weekend newspapers for coupons, and cut them out. Carry them with you so you have them when you need them.

2. Stir in the arrowroot powder and blend well.

3. Add a few drops of rose oil (or another scent) for extra fragrance.

4. Pour the powder into an airtight container. Decorate the container by tying a bow around the container and lid.

5. Attach a little card to the bow with directions for use: "To use, dab a cotton ball into the powder and apply to body."

Rose Petal Perfume

What You Need

fresh rose or carnation petals
(you can purchase a dozen roses from your local discount store for only a few dollars)

ribbon

funnel

colander

small bowl

small glass jar (1 oz. or smaller)

water

What to Do

1. Gather fresh petals. Wash and dry them.

2. Fill a small jar with petals until the jar is completely full.

3. Fill the jar with water, then tightly screw on the lid and let the jar set for 3 to 4 weeks.

4. Strain the liquid through a colander into a small bowl.

5. Pour the perfume through a funnel into a small glass jar or perfume bottle.

6. Add a ribbon and tag that reads "Rose Petal Perfume."

7. Sell as a gift item for birthdays, holidays and anniversaries.

✳ **Make a sample jar so customers can sample your product without having to wait three or four weeks.**

BASIL HAIR RINSE

Tell your customers this homemade hair rinse will leave their hair shiny and clean, removing all traces of soap!

What You Need

¼ cup basil and/or rosemary leaves

½ cup white vinegar

small saucepan

mixing bowl

colander

funnel

8 oz. jar

What to Do

1. Place the basil and/or rosemary leaves in the jar.

2. Ask an adult to help you heat the vinegar in a small saucepan at low heat for 5 minutes. Don't let it boil!

3. Let the adult pour the vinegar into the jar, over the herbs.

4. Replace the lid on the jar and put it in a cool, dark place for one week.

5. Open the jar and strain the liquid through a colander into a mixing bowl. Throw away the herbs.

6. Pour the liquid back into the jar, then put enough water into the jar to fill it.

7. Tie a tag around the bottle with these instructions: "Use after you shampoo for clean, shiny hair."

Tip Jar!

❋ **Let the customers smell the product.**

❋ **Contact local health food stores to see if you can sell your product there.**

❋ **Offer suggestions for buying the rinse, such as for a wedding shower gift or as a new mom "welcome home" surprise!**

ROSE AND LAVENDER BATH LIQUID

Here's a cozy treat for after a hard day at school or work! Make extra as a gift for your mom or someone special.

What You Need

1 cup red rose petals

1 cup lavender petals

(rose and lavender petals can be purchased at natural food stores, craft stores and online)

4 cups white vinegar

12 oz. pretty glass jar

(try finding different shapes and sizes at yard sales or at the dollar or craft store)

mixing bowl

funnel

saucepan

measuring cup

What to Do

1. Fill the glass jar with the rose and lavender petals.

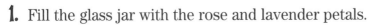

2. Pour the vinegar into a saucepan and ask an adult to heat it on low. Don't let it boil!

3. Let the adult pour the hot vinegar into the jar over the petals. Replace the jar's lid and store it in a cool, dark place for a week.

4. Strain the petals from the liquid by pouring the liquid through a colander into a mixing bowl. Throw away the petals.

5. Pour the vinegar back into the bottle and replace the lid.

6. Tie a ribbon around the bottle and attach a card with these instructions: "To use, add ½ cup while running your bath. Enjoy!"

Tip Jar!

❊ **Offer to gift wrap the bottle for an additional fee.**

❊ **Take orders for these before the holidays and always have one to show!**

EASY SCENTS

Jesus' friends took scented potpourri to the tomb where Jesus laid after He died on the cross. Since Bible times, essential oils have been added to potpourri and handmade soaps to enhance their fragrance.

What You Need

½ **ounce lavender, spearmint, peppermint, lemon balm or chamomile leaves** *(you can find these at a natural food store, craft store or grocery store)*

4-oz. glass jar (any shape or color)

4 ounces olive oil

colander

What to Do

1. Cut fresh, clean leaves from the herb of your choice.
2. Tightly pack the leaves into a small jar.
3. Pour olive oil into the jar and replace the lid. Keep the jar in a cool, dark place for about three weeks.
4. Strain the oil to remove the leaves.
5. Pour the oil back into the bottle.

✳ Keep a sample of every scent you have so customers can smell them before they buy or place an order.

✳ Sell the oils as they are or create more products by adding oil to potpourri or unscented soap.

✳ The oils can also be added to bath water, but just use a few drops.

HERBAL BATH BAGS

Tell your customers to add these to their bath and breathe in the heavenly fragrances!

What You Need

fresh lavender, rose petals or lemon balm leaves

wavy scissors

8-inch square fabric

ribbon

What to Do

1. Lay the piece of cloth flat, then fill the center with a handful of fresh herbs.

2. Lift the four corners of the fabric and bundle them together. Tie the bundle closed with a piece of ribbon.

3. Add a card with the directions for use: "Drop this herbal bath bag into a tub of hot water and climb in!"

Tip Jar!

✳ **Add colorful ribbons tied in bows.**

✳ **Combine and sell with other herbal products as a "gift set."**

PARTY PLANNER

If you are organized and like people, party planning may be the business for you.

What You Need

calendar

What to Do

1. Decide on the services you want to offer. Most party planners are in charge of a party from start to finish.

That means you will come up with a theme, set up, run the party and clean up. Do you want to charge by the hour or a flat fee?

2. Make colorful flyers advertising your services and post them at party stores, schools and libraries. You especially want to target busy parents who need someone to handle their kids' birthday parties.

3. When a customer calls, have a calendar ready so you can write down the date and time of the party. Discuss the theme with the customer, and the number and ages of people expected. Also discuss your fees and what the customer wants to spend on supplies for the party.

4. Decide on a place for the party. If you are planning an outdoor party, be sure to have an inside spot, too, in case of rain. Decide how you will arrange chairs and tables.

5. Make up a guest list and a party menu to follow.

6. Buy party invitations or create your own.

7. Send out the invitations 10-14 days before the party.

8. Plan all of the games and entertainment.

9. Make a list of all the party supplies you need to buy.

10. Recruit family and friends to help you set up and/or prepare and serve food, handle games and clean up.

❈ **Team up with friends to help you plan, shop, set up and clean up.**

❈ **Purchase inexpensive, brightly-colored plates, cups, napkins and table coverings at a discount store.**

❈ **Make invitations on your computer to save money.**

❈ **Check out books from the library for games and party ideas.**

PERSONAL PETS

These will sell like hot cakes to pet lovers. And they make a nice add-on product for customers who use your dog walking or grooming services!

What You Need

cat and dog collars

leashes

food and water dishes

permanent markers, assorted colors

glitter glue pens

What to Do

1. Take orders for personalized food and water dishes, and leashes.

2. Using markers and glitter glue pens, write pet names on plastic pet bowls. For a special touch, draw little mice on cat bowls and bones on dog bowls.

3. Draw spots, flowers, swirls or little sayings such as "Good Dog!" or "Bow Wow" or "Cool Cat" on the leashes and collars.

4. Set up a stand at craft fairs and yard sales. Don't forget to bring some change!

Tip Jar!

※ **Make samples so people can see the finished products.**

※ **Offer them as gift ideas at Christmas.**

※ **Also sell pet toys and treats at your stand.**

PeNCIL POWeR

Decorate and sell pencils to share your faith or promote other good causes.

What You Need

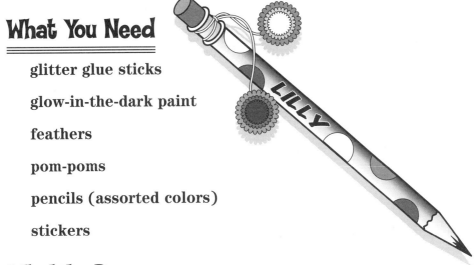

glitter glue sticks

glow-in-the-dark paint

feathers

pom-poms

pencils (assorted colors)

stickers

What to Do

1. Paint Christian symbols (fish, cross, star of David) on pencils and write sayings like "Jesus loves you!"

2. Use glitter, feathers and pom-poms to decorate the pencils.

3. Also take orders for personalized pencils. Customers can tell you the names they want on the pencils and how many they want, or if they want specific colors or special decorations.

Tip Jar!

※ **Think about upcoming holidays and make pencils to go along with the season's colors and themes.**

※ **Tell everyone at school about your business. Bring samples and take orders!**

✳ **Check to see if any schools in your area have stores where you could sell your pencils. Make pencils with school colors and mascots to appeal to those schools.**

✳ **Give a few away for advertising and to get the buzz started.**

✳ **Always be sure to use one yourself so others will ask where you got it!**

PET ROCKS

This 70s fad is back – and crazier than ever!

What You Need

markers

paint, various colors

glitter

brushes

felt

glue

any size smooth stones *(found by a creek or pond or ask your local garden center if they have any you can have for free)*

What to Do

1. Come up with some themes for your Pet Rocks such as actual pets (cats, dogs, hamsters, etc.), Rock of Ages (Christian symbols), Rock Concert (with moppy yarn heads), or Rocking the Cradle (babies with diapers and tiny pacifiers).

2. Paint faces and designs on the stones.

3. Cut felt the same sizes as the stones and glue it on.

4. Add accessories to the rocks, depending on their themes. For example, a cat rock might have a pink fuzzy collar, or a dog rock could have a collar with a leash. Use sequins as eyes and other jewels for facial features.

5. Decide what you will charge for your rocks. They can be different prices depending on the sizes and the amount of decorations each one has.

6. Sell your Pet Rocks at craft fairs.

❊ **Display your rocks using pedestals or colored tissue paper.**

❊ **Find some used jewelry boxes and place pet rocks inside them for protection.**

❊ **Be a teacher's pet and give a pet rock to your favorite teacher!**

READ 'EM AGAIN USED BOOKS

Why let your books just sit on your shelves collecting dust? Make money by selling them!

What You Need

old books

What to Do

1. Gather books that you've read or that your family is no longer using.

2. Take them to a used bookstore. Most used bookstores will let you decide if you want cash for your books or if you'd like to exchange them for books in the store.

✳ **If you see a good deal on books at yard sales, buy them, then sell them to the used bookstore for a profit.**

✳ **Ask neighbors to give you any old books and magazines they plan to throw out.**

✳ **Short on cash for Christmas? Exchange your used books for some to give as Christmas presents. Many used books look like new!**

READY TO RECYCLE

Help improve the environment and make money at the same time.

What You Need

wagon

garbage bags

What to Do

1. Ask neighbors, friends and relatives to let you have all of their cans and newspapers.

2. Choose one day of the week to pick up the recyclables from your customers.

3. Once you have a large stack of newspapers and several garbage bags filled with cans, ask your mom or dad to take you to a recycling center in your area.

4. The recycling center will pay you by the pound for what you give them.

❈ **Find out what the hours of operation are at your local recycling center.**

❈ **Distribute flyers to local businesses and restaurants (where there is a lot of trash!).**

❈ **Ask drink machine owners if you can leave a box marked CANS for recycling by their machines.**

❈ **Recyclable aluminum includes cans, pie pans, aluminum siding and window frames.**

❈ **Ask neighbors if you can leave boxes at their houses and then pick them up at the end of the week.**

RUNAROUND YOU!

Help your parents and neighbors save time by starting an errand service.

What You Need

poster board

pens

markers

memo pad

bike, backpack
or wagon

What to Do

1. Decide how to charge for your service. You could charge one fee per delivery or base it on the distance you need to travel.

2. Make flyers to announce your new business. Pass them out and hang them up around your neighborhood. Some ideas for services: returning library books, getting gas for lawn equipment, buying groceries or picking up dry cleaning.

3. Your bicycle is probably your best bet for pick-ups and deliveries, but a backpack or wagon could work, too, depending how far you need to go.

❊ **Keep a memo pad with you at all times so you can write down tasks, directions and any other important information.**

❊ **Try to group your errands so you are not making multiple trips. For example, travel to the library once every few days rather than going for every customer.**

 **SAVE-A-LOT COUPON BOOKS**

You can make money without even selling a product. How? With this free coupon book that includes paid ads!

What You Need

computer

paper

printer

What to Do

1. Figure out how many households will receive your coupon book.

2. Call and/or visit local businesses and tell them you are making coupon books to sell (bring a sample). Let them know you will be distributing the books free to local residents' homes and to stores.

3. Charge each advertiser for a ⅛ spot on a page.

4. Use a computer to design and make your book's pages.

5. Have the booklets printed at a local printer or copy center. Have the copy center print 8 coupons per page and staple the booklets together.

6. Distribute the booklets to stores or go door-to-door and drop them off.

7. Be sure each advertiser receives a book.

✳ **If an advertiser is not ready to pay for an ad when you first visit, accept half the fee at that time and the second half when you deliver the finished coupon booklet.**

✳ **Make sure to put your business name and telephone number inside the booklets so other advertisers can call you for future editions.**

✳ **In addition to money-saving coupons, try selling informational ads for club meetings, instructional studios and political candidates.**

SCHOOL SPIRIT PENNANTS

When football season begins, you can be ready with these custom flags. Display them at school. Take orders, then deliver after school.

What You Need

felt, variety of colors

scissors

glue

paint

tassels

What to Do

1. Find out the colors and mascots for all the schools in your area.

2. To make a pennant, cut a long triangle shape out of felt, using one of the school's colors.

3. Use letter stencils to cut out the school's name (or initials) from the school's other color.

4. Glue the letters onto the pennant.

5. Add tassels to the edges.

6. Add other decorations if there is space, such as bows, bells, pom-poms or items related to the school's mascot (such as a fur-fabric paw for "Tigers" or a beaded ribbon for "Indians").

※ **Sell other items with the schools' colors such as pens, pencils, ribbons and stickers.**

※ **Hang one on your school locker as an advertisement.**

※ **Recruit sponsors by getting friends in your Pep Club to tell everyone!**

SUMMERTIME SPORTS CAMP

In the middle of summer when moms are tired and kids are bored, you can offer them this fun service. And you'll get some sun and exercise, too!

What You Need

sports equipment *(jump ropes, bats, kickballs, Wiffle™ balls, volleyballs, tetherballs, croquet sets, badminton sets)*

cooler with water, soda and ice

a flat water slide

Frisbees™

What to Do

1. Plan your camp. Will it be one day or several days or even weeks?

2. Decide which sports you will offer on which days and write out a schedule (leave room for a break halfway through the day for kids to rest). Limit your camp to about three hours per day.

3. Figure out how many kids you can handle by yourself, or recruit friends to help you.

4. Come up with a pricing plan for the camp. Will you charge one fee for the whole day or charge by the hour? Will you give campers who come more than one day a discount? Could families who bring more than one child get a discount?

5. Make flyers advertising your sports camp and hang them around your neighborhood, at schools, in libraries and at sports stores. Be sure to include your name and phone number, the camp's name, the dates and times for each day of camp, where it will be held, what it will cost and the ages of kids you will accept.

6. When parents call to register their children, get their names and phone numbers. Tell them what time the camp begins and ends, and tell them what the child should bring such as a snack, or swimsuit and towel.

✳ **If you don't have a water slide, you can make your own using a long plastic tarp. Wet it well, then have a friend sit on each corner to hold it down.**

✳ **If you get a lot of campers, go to a wholesale club or discount store so you can buy more drinks at cheaper prices.**

✳ **A related business idea for a sporty business: be an exercise partner for someone who is training for a particular sport.**

TeRRIFIC TUToR

Tutor kids who need help with their homework by providing this after-school service.

What You Need

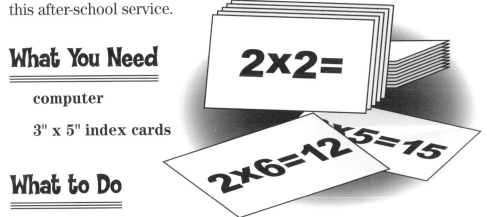

computer

3" x 5" index cards

What to Do

1. In which school subjects do you excel? Make a list of possibilities.

2. Decide what you will charge. An hourly rate is probably best for this service. Give families with more than one child a special rate.

3. Write your name, phone number and the types and costs of services you will offer on index cards. Post the cards on bulletin boards at libraries and schools. Pass them out around your neighborhood.

4. When you get a call, write down the name, address and phone number of your customer, and the appointment time.

5. At the tutoring sessions, go over the students' lessons. Have the students practice while you correct them.

6. Be positive and tell your students what they do right – don't just correct their mistakes.

※ **Always be patient with your students. It may take a while for them to understand the lessons.**

※ **Bring books and games to help them learn in different ways.**

※ **Get each student a treat for after your session. They will love you!**

※ **If you are good at computers, offer to tutor adults to use computers or software.**

THAT'S NEWS TO ME!

No matter what your interests are, the sky's the limit to what you can do in the publishing industry.

What You Need

computer

printer

paper

clip art

word processing software

What to Do

1. Choose a theme, such as sports, religion or collecting. Or publish a newsletter about your neighborhood (events, lost pets, new neighbors, etc.).

2. Ask friends and family for story ideas and try writing about some of them. You also could ask friends to submit their own articles.

3. Decide whether to publish monthly or weekly.

4. Ask local businesses to advertise in your newsletter, especially those that might be interested in your topic. Charge for each ad that is placed.

5. Your word processing software should have newsletter templates built into it. If so, use a template so your newsletter will look professional. Also use clip art and photos when possible to add visual color.

6. Sell subscriptions to those whom the newsletter would interest.

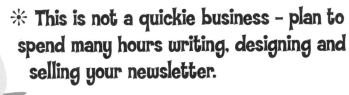

❊ **This is not a quickie business – plan to spend many hours writing, designing and selling your newsletter.**

❊ **Make sure you have an audience and people interested in the subject you choose, otherwise you won't sell ads or newsletters!**

❊ **Ask a business to print the newsletter for free by offering to let them advertise for free.**

Green Back FACT

For a fun night, rent the movie "Where the Red Fern Grows." It's a sweet story about a boy who achieves his dreams by hard work and tough determination. You will be inspired to work harder to achieve your own goals and dreams!

TIME-SAVING TYPIST

If you have a computer, you can earn big bucks by typing papers and book reports for your less keyboard-capable customers.

What You Need

computer

word processing software

What to Do

1. Decide what to charge for your service. Most typists charge by the page rather than by the hour or project, but do what's right for you.

2. Make flyers and posters and distribute them at schools, libraries and copy centers. Don't forget local colleges!

3. When customers call, write down when they will be dropping off their papers and when they need them returned.

4. Ask customers how their papers should be formatted, such as margins, line spacing, font size and so on.

5. Be sure to collect your payment before giving the paper to the customer.

❋ Tell all your school friends!

❋ Advertise using flyers at the local library and grocery store.

WATCH YOUR MONEY GROW WATERING CAN

Who says money doesn't grow on trees? Here's a way to help the environment by turning a detergent bottle into something to sell.

What You Need

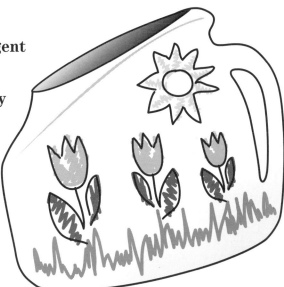

plastic liquid detergent bottle (any size)

acrylic paint, variety of colors

paintbrush

old newspapers

poster board

markers

What to Do

1. Make sure the detergent bottle is clean and soap-free. Don't worry about trying to remove the label – you will paint over it.

2. Cover your workspace with old newspapers, and wear old clothing.

3. Paint the entire label with blue paint to create a sky background. Allow to dry.

4. Using the brown paint, make a boat in the lower half portion of the sky background.

5. Paint a rainbow using all the other colors around the boat and sky. Allow to dry.

6. Use the black paint to outline the rainbow.

7. Paint a swirly border around your artwork with the red paint.

8. Make flyers with a picture of your product to pass out and leave on your neighbors' doors.

❋ **Ask neighbors for empty detergent bottles to use.**

❋ **Sell to garden clubs or to church women's groups.**

❋ **Sell at craft shows, or door-to-door in the spring.**

WIDE-EYED PHOTOGRAPHY

Take pictures at sporting events or parties so others are free to enjoy the fun.

What You Need

digital camera

laptop computer

printer

paper

markers

photo paper

What to Do

1. Charge by the hour to cover the costs of your equipment and supplies.

2. Hang flyers around your neighborhood, and at schools and party stores.

3. When a customer calls, get his or her name and phone number, when the event is, where it is and what time it starts.

4. Arrive about an hour early to set up your equipment and meet the hosts.

5. Set up the camera and computer so the customers can see the photos right away and decide which ones they want. (Practice this at home first so you have the hang of it!)

Tip Jar!

✳ **Dress appropriately for the party or event.**

✳ **Make sure that you take pictures of all the guests, not just the same few.**

✳ **Carry business cards to give to people who may ask about your service.**

✳ STAR PATTERNS ✳

✳ BUSINESS CARD PATTERN ✳

☀ MY MONTHLY BUDGET ☀

Money Earned

Allowance $_____

Gifts $_____

Business Income $_____

Extra Chores $_____

Other Income $_____

Money Spent

Business Expenses $_____

Things For Me $_____

School/Class Supplies $_____

God's Work (tithes) $_____

Other Expenses $_____

Total Money Earned $ _____

Total Money Spent $ _____ (- minus)

What's Leftover $ _____

What to do with what's leftover:

Savings $_____

God's Work $_____

Major Purchase $_____

Other $_____

☀ WEEKLY SCHEDULE ☀

	Sun	Mon	Tues	Wed	Thurs	Fri	Sat
7 am							
8 am							
9 am							
10 am							
11 am							
Noon							
1 pm							
2 pm							
3 pm							
4 pm							
5 pm							
6 pm							
7 pm							
8 pm							
9 pm							
10 pm							

☀ WHAT TO CHARGE ☀

First, figure out what you will spend to make each item...

Supplies $_____

Advertising $_____

Equipment $_____

Other Stuff $_____

Total Expenses $_____

Next, figure out what your time will cost for the job...

My time is worth $_____ (per hour)

It takes me _____ hours to make each item or provide the service.

Total Time Cost $_____ (per hour fee x number of hours)

Then add those two together...

Total Expenses $_____ +

Total Time Cost $_____

Total Cost to You $_____

Now, decide how much profit you want to make. Usually, you can charge three or four times what the item or job costs you. For example, if it costs you 25 cents to make an item, you can charge $1 to your customers.

Desired Profit $_____

To get the final price for your item or service, add together the Total Cost to You and Desired Profit...

Total Cost to You $_____

Desired Profit $_____

Final Price $_____

❋ BUSINESS PLAN ❋

My business's name: _____

What my business sells or does: _____

What are my business's hours: _____

Who are my customers: _____

How I will advertise: _____

How I will find customers: _____

Prices of my products or services: _____

List the benefits of my product: _____

To-do List

1. _____

2. _____

3. _____

4. _____

5. _____

Supplies Needed   Cost?

1. _____

2. _____

3. _____

4. _____

5. _____

☀ CUSTOMER RECEIPT ☀

Business Name: _____

Address: _____

Phone Number: _____

Customer Name: _____

Date: _____

Customer Address: _____

Phone: _____

Description _____

_____

_____

Price: _____

Total: _____

✳ DOOR HANGER PATTERN ✳

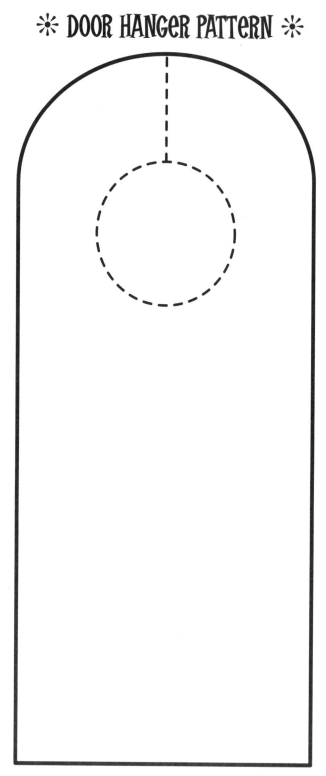